Hercules Mulligan

Confidential Correspondent of General George Washington – A Son of Liberty in the American War of Independence

By Michael J. O'Brien

PANTIANOS
CLASSICS

Published by Pantianos Classics

ISBN-13: 978-1-78987-132-6

First published in 1937

Contents

Chapter One 5

Chapter Two 10

Chapter Three 16

Chapter Four 22

Chapter Five 28

Chapter Six 35

Chapter Seven 40

Chapter Eight 45

Chapter Nine 51

Chapter Ten 56

Chapter Eleven 62

Chapter Twelve 68

Chapter Thirteen 74

Chapter Fourteen 79

Appendices 85

Appendix One - To Charlotte Mulligan 85

Appendix Two - Breakfast with Hercules Mulligan 86

Appendix Three - Narrative of Hercules Mulligan 88

Inscription on Vault in Trinity Churchyard

Chapter One

ALONG the toilsome route that I have travelled, in search of the story of the Irish pioneers in America, I have picked up many interesting fragments of information concerning individual Irishmen which seem to deserve a place in American history. In local annals of the colonial and revolutionary periods, there are sometimes noted instances of men, covered perhaps with vicarious glory, whose names have become household words in the communities where they lived; while in the case of others not less worthy, their activities in the public affairs of the day are almost wholly forgotten or unknown.

Of the last mentioned, we find an instance in the person of Hercules Mulligan, a resident of the City of New York for many years before the Revolution, who was active in the political agitation which preceded that momentous conflict, not only as a member of the Sons of Liberty, but of several important Revolutionary Committees, and who ran the risk of prying into the movements of the enemy and conveying the information to the opposing forces. Why a man of this stamp has remained in obscurity cannot readily be understood, but perhaps the cause may be attributed either to a sense of modesty on the part of the individual himself, who eschewed notoriety, or to the failure of the historians of the Revolution to examine the public records and accord him the credit to which he was entitled. However that may be, the name and fame of Hercules Mulligan are almost entirely unknown in this, the City of his home for more than three quarters of a century, and where he was known and respected by the best elements in the community.

The Mulligan family has occupied a definite place in Irish history. O'Hart in his *Irish Pedigrees* says they were originally a Tyrone clan. He enumerates them among "The Principal Families of Ulster" and refers to O'Mulligan as "Chief of the territory of MacCarthney," in the County of Derry. Irish genealogists also show that in ancient days the heads of the sept were Princes of Moyliffey and that their possessions were located in the Counties of Derry, Mayo and Cavan. O'Hart also locates them in Cavan and couples them with the O'Dalys and O'Farrellys as "hereditary bards and historians to O'Reilly." The O'Mulligans, in fact, are enumerated among the "Bardic families of Ireland" as far back as the ninth century.

In ancient Ireland it was a very high honor to be enrolled among the Bards, and it is interesting to note that in the institutions of the country the Bards held a rank equal to the princes and chief nobility. For example, the Bards and Brehons were privileged to dine with the King, and as a mark of distinction they were permitted to wear six colors in their garments, the Kings themselves not wearing more than six, while military commanders and other public officers, according to their rank and dignities, wore only five, four, three or two colors, as the case might be. From this we see that the

O'Mulligans were no "common people" in their native country. There are those who seem to think that the name has anything but a classic sound, and possibly there were Mulligans themselves in Ireland who were of the same way of thinking, for some of the descendants of the ancient line now bear such anglicized forms of the name as Molyneux and Milligan. It is evident, however, that these names had no special attraction for the branch of the family to which Hercules Mulligan belonged, for except for the dropping of the prefix "O," they adhered to the name handed down by their ancestors.

A few years ago I wrote a short account of Hercules Mulligan for a New York newspaper, and many persons then enquired "if his given name really were Hercules," forgetful of the fact that it was not uncommon for some Irish families a century or more ago to give biblical or Grecian Christian names to their children. The fact that he was baptized Hercules would seem to indicate that his father was familiar with Grecian mythology and probably was something of a scholar. In the genealogies of other Irish families, occasional instances are noted of the use of the name Hercules, and of other mythical heroes of ancient days. The name is suggestive of great strength, and indeed Hercules Mulligan's record during the War of the Revolution was quite in consonance with his name, for he proved himself a fearless patriot and a man of great determination and strength of character. It is evident then that he was not inappropriately named, since he is known to have been a man of large stature, and in one of the volumes of *Valentine's Manual,* there is a reference to Hercules' son, Colonel John W. Mulligan, who commanded the Fifth New York regiment in 1809, wherein the writer speaks of him as "a man of large proportions and sturdy fibre." A grandson, Henry Strong Mulligan, is also spoken of in the family as a man of fine physique and imposing presence, and there is a portrait of Charlotte Mulligan, great-granddaughter of Hercules, in the Twentieth Century Club at Buffalo, N. Y., of which she was the founder, which shows her to have been a woman of fine proportions and a refined but determined countenance.

Comparatively little is known of his early life or parentage. But, according to family records preserved by his great-granddaughter, Mrs. Ellen Mulligan Fanning of Flushing, New York, and by his great-grandson, Edward Howell Mulligan of Pasadena, California, he was born on September 25, 1740, at Coleraine, County Antrim, to which place it is said his grandfather removed in the late years of the seventeenth century. One of his descendants has said that "the family came from Blarney, County Cork," but that undoubtedly was an error, for it is known that the Mulligans were an old Connaught and Ulster clan. There were Mulligans enrolled in the Society of **United Irishmen,** who took part in the Rebellion of 1798, and one of the name belonging to a body of the patriots organized in Antrim, was wounded and captured at the battle of Saintfield in that County in June, 1798.

Doubtless, this soldier of freedom was one of the Coleraine family, and I venture to say that, like his kinsman, Hercules was also early imbued with that hatred of British rule which has been grounded into Irish hearts by centuries of oppression. There may have been some tradition in the American branch of the family, that prior to their advent in this country they lived for a time in the town of Blarney, or that they sailed for this country from the nearby port of Cork, which would create the impression that he was a native of that section of the country. Indeed, it would almost seem that before leaving Ireland, Hercules must have kissed some good substitute for the Blarney Stone, if not the original, for he had an unmistakable "touch of the Blarney" in his make-up, which he put to good use in after years in pursuit of the dangerous post of "confidential correspondent of General Washington."

The genealogical data in the possession of his American descendants show that Hercules' grandfather and father were both named Hugh, and that the latter married Sarah Cooke in Ireland. They had three sons, Hugh, Hercules and Cooke, and one daughter, Sarah, all except Cooke born in Coleraine. The precise time of the emigration of the family from Ireland is somewhat in doubt, and it does not seem possible now to ascertain the date from any public records, owing to the absence of emigration statistics. However, their descendants who have kept in touch with the family history inform me that they are thought to have arrived here "about the year 1746," and we do know that Hercules and his elder brother and sister were settled with their parents in the City of New York when quite young. At the Vestry House of Trinity Parish there is a record of the burial in Trinity Churchyard, on October 13, 1777, of Mrs. Sarah Mulligan, mother of Hercules, at the age of eighty. [1]

In a "List of Freemen of the City in the year 1747," now in the custody of the City Clerk, the name was written "Mullaghan," when Hugh Mulligan was registered as a "Freeman" on November 3rd, 1747. [2] There can be no doubt that this was the father of Hercules, and the fact that Hugh was made a "Freeman" as early as 1747, in itself is an indication that he was a man of substance and some standing in the community, and it is evident also that the family did not come over as "redemptioners," but were able to pay their own way.

The "Minutes of the Meetings of the Common Council of the City of New York" show that at a meeting of the Council held on October 14th, 1748, Hugh Mulligan was appointed "Deputy Constable for the Dock Ward"; during the succeeding six years, at the annual meetings of the Council in September, he was appointed to the same office, and on October 14th, 1756, he took the oath of office as "Constable of the Dock Ward" before Recorder Simon Johnson. [3] The "Poll List of New York on Election for Assembly, February, 1761," [4] contains the name of Hugh Mulligan. Beyond this, little is known of the parents, or of the descendants, if any, of Hercules' brothers, although several persons of the name are mentioned in New York records of the eighteenth century, who may possibly have been of this family.

In 1747 Hugh Mulligan was in business as a "peruke maker," but, in later years he was engaged in mercantile business, and all three of his sons received a commercial training and became prosperous merchants. His son, Hugh, was married to Catherine Pool on March 8, 1760. [5] In a "List of New York Merchants on the Roll of Freemen, 1769," appears the name, Cooke Mulligan, and the date of his admission as a "Freeman" is shown by the records of the Common Council as January 31st, 1769. [6] and in 1772 he was made an honorary member of "The Marine Society of the City of New York." It is evident that the family was well brought up, for in Holt's *New York Journal or General Advertiser* of February 29th, 1776, in announcing the death of Hercules' brother, Cooke, the editor said: "On Wednesday the 21 st, died Mr. Cooke Mulligan of this City, Merchant, a young Gentleman whose amiable Disposition and exemplary Character endeared him to all his Acquaintances, who, while they regret their own Loss, rejoice in the firm Persuasion of his Existence in a State of permanent Happiness." It was a matter of some distinction in those days for a newspaper editor to make such laudatory reference to any man, living or dead, and a comparison of the lists of New York marriages and deaths shows an exceedingly small percentage of such happenings mentioned in the colonial newspapers.

Shortly after the arrival of the family in New York, Hercules was placed under the care of Master James O'Brien, whose school was in Horse and Cart Street, now that part of William Street south of Wall. Master O'Brien was one of several Irish schoolmasters, who, at that time were established in this City, some of them in the immediate neighborhood of the Mulligan home. While on this point, I would say, parenthetically, that for a work now in course of preparation on Ireland's contribution to American education, I have gathered the records of those early Irish schoolmasters, and while it may be a surprise to many to say, that great numbers of the colonial youth were educated by these "old country" teachers, there is unquestionable evidence of its historic truth. Several of the teachers to whom New York youth were indebted more or less for their education were graduates of Dublin's celebrated University. As early as 1726, Revd. James Colgan, an Irish Protestant clergyman, conducted the "Charity School" attached to Trinity Church, and in 1746 he was succeeded by Revd. Richard Charlton, a graduate of Trinity College, Dublin, [7] and who, according to the College records, was born in Longford, Ireland, in the year 1705. [8] Robert Harper, a native of Ireland, who was a professor at King's College between 1761 and 1776, is referred to as "one of the most distinguished educators in the Province." William Cockran, a native of Tyrone, Master of the Grammar School at Columbia College, is credited in history as the tutor of the celebrated Virginia statesman, John Randolph of Roanoke, [9] and when Cockran hired an assistant for his school in 1784 he announced that he had "secured the services of George Wright, an Irishman, and a graduate of Trinity College, Dublin." While among the Irish schoolmasters who imparted to New York youth their earliest lessons were: Thomas Flynn in 1704; Miles Reilly in 1734; Cornelius Lynch and James Magrath, whose schools were in Stone and Dock Streets respectively in 1740; Edward

Fogarty and James Carroll, who kept schools in Wall Street after 1766; James Farrell and James Gilliland in Broad Street; Patrick Coffey in Nassau Street; James Foley in Duke Street, and James Barry, who had a classical school on Golden Hill. And after the Revolution, that is, between 1784 and 1791, there are records of New York schoolmasters named Brennan, Carney, Connery, Connoly, Conroy, Duffy, Finnegan, Gahagan, Gillespie, Heffernan, Joyce, Kearns, McDonald, McDonnel, McKiernan, Madden, O'Brien, O'Connor, Piggot, Reilly, Sweeney, Patrick Murdock [10] and others, whose schools were located in the present downtown portion of the City, and whose names are an obvious indication of their nationality. [11]

In the case of Hercules Mulligan, there is some reason for assuming that he was a fairly well educated youth, according to the standards of the day. And the fact that in 1775 he was appointed a member of the Revolutionary Committee of Correspondence of the City of New York, in itself indicates that he was a man of some education. His first employment seems to have been with an importing house on the water front, then the principal business section of the City. He was an ambitious youth with plenty of energy at his command, and to this may be attributed the success which he achieved in after life. I am unable to determine when he began business on his own account, but it is probable that it was before 1765, and his name is listed among a number of citizens who appeared before the Common Council and "on application took the Freeman's oath and were admitted Freemen" on October 1st, of that year. [12] And in a copy of "The Poll List of the Election for Representatives for the City and County of New York," of the years 1768 and 1769, in the records of the Common Council, Hercules Mulligan's name appears, showing the candidates for whom he voted.

[1] *Register of Burials in the Parish of Trinity Church;* Vol. i.
[2] See *Manual of the Corporation of the City of New York,* compiled by David T. Valentine.
[3] *Minutes;* Vol. 6, p. 66.
[4] In James Grant Wilson's *History of the City of New York;* Vol. 2, p. 321.
[5] Marriage Bonds, office of Secretary of State; Vol. 3, p. 70.
[6] *New York Historical Society Collections;* Vol. for 1885, p. 127.
[7] *New York Gazette and Weekly Mercury,* October 13, 1777.
[8] Letter from the Librarian, Trinity College, Dublin, December 31, 1924.
[9] Garland's *Life of John Randolph.*
[10] Patrick Murdock was tutor to Mrs. Martha Washington's grandchildren at his school in New York in 1790. See *Private Affairs of George Washington—from the Records and Accounts of Tobias Leary his private Secretary,* ed. by Stephen Decatur; Boston, Mass., 1933.
[11] These names have been obtained from numerous authoritative sources, including the New York newspapers of the time. The names of most of these schoolmasters are also listed in the City Directories after 1786.
[12] See *New York Historical Society Collections;* Vol. for 1885, p. 203.

Chapter Two

ABOUT the time the agitation over the Stamp Act began, Mulligan was a sturdy young Irishman, and, as events proved, he was no lover of British rule, so there is nothing surprising in the fact that he early identified himself with the association known as the "Sons of Liberty." I rather imagine it was the sort of organization that appealed to his Celtic temperament. Like so many of his countrymen, the "troubled sea of politics" was consonant with his nature, and he seems to have entered upon it with zeal and found in this field an outlet for that exuberance of spirit which manifested itself through the whole course of his life. He is said to have been a participant in the fight between the "Liberty Boys" and English soldiers on Golden Hill (now that part of John Street, west of William), on the 18th of January, 1770, where the first blood of the American Revolution was shed. [1] From Game's *New York Gazette and Weekly Mercury* of March 25th, 1771, we learn that "the association was formed to celebrate the repeal of the Stamp Act of 1765," and according to Holt's *New York Journal or General Advertiser* of December 16th, 1773, "the Association of the Sons of Liberty was comprised of a great Number of the principal Gentlemen of the City, Merchants, Lawyers and other inhabitants of all Ranks," who organized "to testify their Abhorrence to the Diabolical Project of enslaving America."

It is a noteworthy fact that it was an Irishman who suggested the name of the association. In the debate on the Stamp Act in the British Parliament on February 7, 1765, Charles Townshend, Chancellor of the Exchequer, concluded his speech on the bill with this peroration: "And now will these Americans, children planted by our care, nourished up by our indulgence, until they are grown to a degree of strength and opulence, and protected by our arms, will they grudge to contribute their mite to relieve us from the heavy weight of that burden which we lie under." Colonel Isaac Barre, an Irish member, immediately responded. With eyes emitting fire and outstretched arm, and with a truly prophetic vision, Barré delivered one of the most remarkable speeches of his career, in which he characterized the American patriots as "those Sons of Liberty," to the utter consternation of the House!

In the gallery of the House, during the debate on the Stamp Act, sat Jared Ingersoll, the agent of Connecticut, who, delighted with Barre's sentiments, sent a report of his speech to the New London *Gazette*, which printed it in its issue of May 10, 1765. It was reprinted in the Newport, R. I., *Mercury* of May 27th, and in the Boston Gazette of August 27, 1765. Thence, it was copied far and wide, and Barre's famous phrase, Sons of Liberty, which had fallen so naturally from his lips, became the rallying cry of the American patriots. Such was the origin of the name of the "Sons of Liberty." [2] Barre was a member of an old family domiciled in Ireland since the Norman invasion of 1172; he was born in Dublin in 1728 and died in 1802. He had much knowledge of

American affairs, having served through the French-English war, and while a member of the British Parliament, like his countryman, Edmund Burke, "he was ever the champion of American freedom." [3]

Readers of American history are well acquainted with the correspondence between Benjamin Franklin and Charles Thomson [4] of Philadelphia in relation to the Stamp Act. On the very day the Act was passed Franklin wrote to Thomson: "The sun of liberty is set, the Americans must now light up the candles of industry and economy/' and the distinguished Irishman's reply to Franklin: that he "was apprehensive that other lights would be the consequence," soon rang like an alarum bell in every town and settlement, and today is written in American annals as one of the most prophetic utterances of that historic time!

The accounts published in the newspapers of the years 1765-6 are highly interesting, as indicating the trend of public opinion in America at that period. Much space was given to reports of meetings of the Sons of Liberty in various parts of the country, especially in the City of New York, and to letters on the Stamp Act from indignant patriots. For several months after the Act went into effect, resolutions protesting against it kept pouring into New York and other cities where newspapers were published. Hugh Gaine published some of them in the *Mercury,* and the accounts printed in this paper of meetings of the association in New York plainly show that many people were worked up to a high pitch of excitement over the iniquities of the Stamp Act, and that they constantly demanded its repeal.

The earliest indication of Mulligan's activities as a patriot was in connection with the circulation of a weekly paper called *The Constitutional Courant.* This paper was started at Woodbridge, N. J., in 1765, with the avowed object of opposing the Stamp Act, and in order to deceive the authorities, the publisher announced that it was "printed at the Sign of the Bribe refused, on Constitution Hill in North America!" Copies were sent secretly to the Sons of Liberty in New York, and it became a question as to how it could be distributed among the citizens without the knowledge of the authorities. Several declined the proposition to handle it, but Hercules Mulligan soon found a willing agent in the person of Lawrence Sweeney, at that time New York's only letter carrier and known popularly as "the Penny Post Boy," and who had previously been in the employ of Kortright and Company, in which concern Hugh Mulligan was then junior partner. The government officials, after a vain effort to trace the paper to its source, hailed Sweeney before a Council meeting in the fort, and putting him on the grill for his "traitorous conduct," they demanded that he tell "where that incendiary paper was printed." The bristling bayonets of the soldiers evidently had no terrors for the newsboy; he had no thought of betraying his friend, Mulligan, and in the most perfectly guileless manner he could assume, Sweeney answered: "At Peter Hassenclever's iron works, somewhere in the Jerseys, plase yer honor!" [5] The quick wit of the Irish newsboy caught the fancy of patriotic publishers, and afterwards, other publications of a like kind appeared frequently with the shibboleth, "Printed at Peter Hassenclever's iron works." That Sweeney must have been a popular character in New York, would appear from the following announcement of his death in the *New York Gazette and Weekly Mercury* of April 16, 1770: "Last Tuesday, died Lawrence Sweeney, as well known in this City as any man in it, and will be perhaps as much missed."

The newspapers of the time furnish ample evidence of the sympathy of Hercules Mulligan's countrymen with the cause of the disturbed Colonies. In the Mercury of February 10, 1766, for example, there was an account by Captain Ashmead, master of a vessel which had arrived at Philadelphia from Cork some days before, which said in part: "Captain Ashmead left the Cove of Cork the 12th of December, but brings no later papers from Cork than the 25th of November. The People of Ireland say we are fine Fellows and most heartily wish us Success in our Opposition to the Laws of Tyranny. Their Toast is, *Destruction to the Stamp Act and Success to the free Sons of Liberty in America.* Captain Ashmead says, that it is spoke with great Positiveness that the Stamp Act will be repealed." The *Mercury* on March 31, 1766, also published a despatch from Philadelphia conveying the "agreeable intelligence" that "a vessel was arrived from Cork at Oxford, in Maryland, the Captain of which brought a Cork News Paper in which was a Paragraph taken from one printed in Dublin, containing a letter from a Member of Parliament to his Friend in Ireland dated about the last of January, the Substance of which was, that every Thing relating to the Affairs of America was settled and that the Stamp Act was to be repealed," etc. "These glad Tidings spread a general Joy all over the City, our Bells were set a Ringing, at Night Bonfires were lighted and the Evening was spent most agreeably by the Inhabitants." In the same paper of April 21, 1766, with an account of the arrival of the ship *Hibernia* from Ireland, Gaine published several "extracts of Letters from Londonderry," one of which read: "March 9, this day the Packet brought the agreeable news to this Town of the Stamp Act being repealed, which, be assured, has given us all here infinite pleasure. This goes by the *Hibernia,* Captain Keith, by whom we have the pleasure to inform you of the Repeal of the Stamp Act."

The Act was repealed by the House of Commons on February 22, 1766, and by the House of Lords during the next month, and it is an interesting circumstance that the first account of this welcome news [6] was brought to America in a vessel named the Hibernia, which hailed from an Irish port, and was published in this country in a newspaper edited by an Irishman. The Hibernia sailed from Lough Swilly on March 15, 1766, and the arrival of the vessel at the port of New York was listed among "Vessels registered at the New York Custom House" under date of April 21, 1766. In addition to the significant statements just quoted, there may be seen in the newspapers two letters from Irish merchants in Cork and Dublin to their correspondents in New York and Philadelphia, encouraging the colonists, and a despatch from Philadelphia printed in the *Mercury* of June 2, 1766, said: "From the different parts of Ireland our Accounts are that the Rejoicings, on account of the Repeal of the Stamp Act, were very general as well as very great there." Thus we have first-hand evidence of the strong sympathy exhibited by the people of Ireland toward the patriotic cause in America, and that this feeling was not confined to any particular section of the country. So we need not be surprised to find Irishmen like Hercules Mulligan and his friend, William Mooney, numbered among the "Liberty Boys."

The Sons of Liberty in New York celebrated each year the repeal of the Stamp Act, and in Game's paper of March 25th, 1771, there was an account of "an elegant entertainment" held at a tavern in "The Common" on the evening of March 17th, which was attended by "a great number of the principal Inhabitants of the City, Friends to Liberty and Trade." And that the "Liberty Boys" were on friendly terms with the New York Irish, [7] we may infer from the fact that among the toasts drunk on this occasion was one reading: "Prosperity to Ireland and the Worthy Sons and Daughters of Saint Patrick." On the same evening New York Irishmen were holding their annual celebration of Saint Patrick's Day, and the report in Game's paper of the dinner of the Sons of Liberty said: "Messages of Civil Compliment were exchanged by those Gentlemen and the Friendly Brothers of Saint Patrick who dined at the Queen's Head Tavern." [8]

Hercules Mulligan is not mentioned in any of the public prints prior to the year 1774, at least in so far as can be determined from an examination of the incomplete collection of newspapers at the New York Public Library. The newspapers of that time were issued weekly or semi-monthly; usually they comprised only four pages and were exceedingly sparse about their local City news, and anyone seeking light about old New York from these little sheets will not find it a very easy matter. Perhaps we can realize what sort of newspapers they were from an account of the life of the famous Hugh Gaine, [9] editor and publisher of the New York Gazette and Weekly Mercury. For instance, we are told that "he was an industrious journalist; he not only collected his own news and set up his own types, but he did his own presswork, folded his own papers and delivered them to his subscribers." [10] Much more could hardly be expected from so "industrious" a journalist, so there was little opportunity to get out a very elaborate budget of news.

For some years before the Revolution, and for more than thirty years after its close, Mulligan was established in business in the City of New York, and while, as already stated, the date he started in business is unknown, it is certain that in 1771 he was located on the west side of Smith (now William) Street, in the block between Little Queen and King Streets. [11] In the records of the Register's office of New York County, [12] there is an entry of a deed dated May 9th, 1771, by which "Susannah and Elizabeth Livingston and John W. Smith, executors of the estate of Robert James Livingston, deceased," conveyed to Hercules Mulligan the house and lot on Smith Street which he had occupied for sometime prior to that date. The consideration mentioned in the deed was £1500., as will be seen from a transcript of the document which has been copied from the records in the Register's office. That was a very large sum of money for those days, and since it is hardly possible that Mulligan could have been able to invest so heavily in real estate thus early in his business career, it is probable that, in the transfer of this property, he simply acted as agent for another party, to whom he conveyed it at some later time. [13] This assumption would seem to be borne out by the fact that after 1772 he did not occupy the premises, as he was then in business in Water Street, "next door to Philip Rhinelander's china store, between Burling's Slip and the Fly Market."

Up to 1774, he had not removed from Water Street, since Chief Justice George Shea of the New York Marine Court, in his *Life and Epoch of Alexander Hamilton,* [14] states that "Hamilton lived with Hercules Mulligan in Water Street in 1774," and this statement also appears in a work entitled *Homes of American Statesmen,* [15] published in 1854. [16] Among the wills on file in the office of the Clerk of the Court of Appeals at Albany, there are some wills wherein "Hercules Mulligan, Merchant," is referred to either as executor or legatee, and to the will of "Frances Dennison of New York, Widow," dated September 2, 1784, he signed the attestation clause, "Hercules Mulligan, Merchant."

On October 27, 1773, Mulligan was married in Trinity Church to Elizabeth Sanders, [17] daughter of John Sanders of New York and niece of Admiral Sanders of the British Navy. Ann Sanders, sister of Elizabeth (Sanders) Mulligan, married John William Livingston [18] of the New York family of that name on June 2, 1777, which fact is worthy of notice in that Hercules Mulligan thus became closely allied with a distinguished American family, one of whom, Philip Livingston, was a Signer of the Declaration of Independence. Sarah Mulligan, sister of Hercules, was married at Trinity Church to a New York merchant named Thomas Whaly [19] on June 27, 1751, and among the wills recorded in the Office of the Clerk of the Court of Appeals at Albany is the will of Thomas Whaly, dated September 29, 1780, in which the testator divided his real and personal property among his "wife, Sarah; sons, Thomas and Hercules; daughter, Margaret, and nephew, John Mulligan, son of Hercules Mulligan." He appointed as executors his "wife, Sarah, Cornelius Bogert, Attorney at Law, and brother-in-law, Hercules Mulligan." John Sanders in his will [20] dated April 11, 1787, appointed as executors

his "sons-in-law, Hercules Mulligan, William Parsons and Daniel Dunscomb, [21] Esqr., of New York," and he divided his property among his six children, two of whom he described as "my daughter, Elizabeth, the wife of Hercules Mulligan," and "my daughter, Ann, wife of John William Livingston."

[1] The "Battle of Golden Hill" took place six weeks before the Boston massacre and five years prior to the battle of Lexington, so that New York has reason to claim that in her streets the first blood was shed and the first life sacrificed to the cause of American freedom.

[2] There are many authorities for this statement, among them William Gordon's *History of the Rise, Progress and Establishment of the Independence of the United States* (Vol. i, p. 117); Rufus R. Wilson's *New York Old and New* (Vol. 1, p. 98); Benson J. Lossing's P*ictorial Field Book of the Revolution* (Vol. 1, p. 463); *New York in the American Revolution*, by Wilbur C. Abbott, New York, 1932, and *History of the City of New York*, by Martha J. Lamb, Vol. 1, pp. 716-717; New York, 1877.

[3] So great was the enthusiasm which Barre's speech aroused in this country, that in the next year when the Stamp Act was repealed, the town of Boston had a portrait of him by Stuart hung in Fanueil Hall, but it was destroyed by English soldiers during the siege of Boston in 1776. In a speech in Parliament delivered in March, 1769, Barre predicted the loss of the Colonies, as in his speech on the Stamp Act four years before he predicted the revolt, and during the administration of Lord North he was persistent in his opposition to the obnoxious measures proposed for the government and chastisement of the colonists. It is a significant fact also, that in the same year when Barre delivered his speech on the Stamp Act, it was an Irishman who undertook to distribute the famous "Virginia Resolutions" of 1765. Copies of the Resolutions were handed about in New York in great privacy by the Sons of Liberty, but no printer had the courage to print them. At that time one John McCurdy, a wealthy merchant of Lyme, Conn., was in New York, and after much precaution he was permitted to make a copy of the document, which he carried to New London where it was printed at McCurdy's expense. It was circulated far and wide through New England, and proved eventually the occasion of those disorders which afterwards broke out in the Colonies. This John McCurdy was a native of Ireland, whence he came to New York in the year 1745, subsequently removing to Lyme, Conn. He was a well known patriot of the Revolution—(see *Genealogical and Biographical Monographs,* compiled by Professor and Mrs. Edward E. Salisbury, New Haven, Conn.).

[4] This was Charles Thomson, afterwards Secretary of the Continental Congress. He was a native of the village of Maghera, County Derry, Ireland.

[5] *History of Printing in America* by Isaiah Thomas; Worcester, Mass., 1810. Thomas gave the name of the newsboy as "Samuel" Sweeney, but in the New York newspapers of the time he was referred to as Lawrence, and once as "Larry," and in the entry of his marriage to Martha McDowell at Trinity Church, he was recorded Lawrence Swiney. That he was an Irishman, is indicated by a broadside headed "The Irishman's Petition, written by Lawrence Sweeney," printed in New York in 1769. It was addressed to "the Honorable Commissioners of Excise," and was signed by Patrick O'Connor, Blaney O'Bryan, Carney MacGuire and Lawrence Sweeney.

[6] Some historians say that the first news of the repeal of the Stamp Act reached this country "on a ship owned by John Hancock, which arrived at Boston on May 13, 1766," but the above account from the *New York Mercury* proves that the news was brought by the *Hibernia* nearly a month before.

[7] The Irish constituted no small part of the City's population at this period. In such records as those of the Common Council, the Surrogate's Court, the Register's office, the County Clerk's office, the baptismal, marriage and burial registers of Trinity and other

churches may be seen the names of hundreds of Irish residents of the City. See *In Old New York,* by Michael J. O'Brien; New York, 1928. Another historian remarks: "Nor is it without some small significance that one reads as early as 1768 of those phenomena we associate with much later times, the Irish and the German 'vote,' already making themselves felt in this small but growing metropolis." (*New York in the American Revolution,* by Wilbur C. Abbott, p. 4; N. Y., 1929.)

[8] Afterwards and still known as Fraunces' Tavern.

[9] Hugh Gaine was a native of Belfast, Ireland. He began the publication of this paper in the year 1752. Its name was the Mercury until the year 1767.

[10] *Journalism in the United States,* by Frederic Hudson; New York, 1873.

[11] Now known respectively as Cedar and Pine Streets.

[12] Conveyances; Liber 39, p. 84.

[13] I am unable to find any record of a reconveyance of this property by Hercules Mulligan.

[14] Published in Boston in 1880. This statement is also made by Mrs. Gertrude Atherton in *The Conqueror;* p. 126; New York, 1902.

[15] Page 243.

[16] By Putnam and Co., New York.

[17] Marriage Bonds at Office of Secretary of State; Vol. XXI, p. 148.

[18] *Ibid.,* Vol. XXIV, p. 95.

[19] Thomas Whaly was a native of Donegal, Ireland.

[20] Surrogate's Records, Liber 41, p. 83.

[21] Daniel Dunscomb was a New York lawyer and a patriot of the Revolution. In 1777, he was a member of the General Assembly and in 1779 a member of the Committee of Safety, and after Independence was won he was one of the first citizens of New York to receive a renomination for the Assembly. (Holt's *New York Journal,* July 7, 1777, and December 20, 1783.)

Chapter Three

AS indicating that Mulligan must have been a well-known citizen of New York at this period, the following announcement is quoted from the New York *Gazette and Weekly Mercury* in its issue of October 17th, 1774:

"Public Notice is hereby given to all creditors of John Grumly deceased that they will send in their accounts to the subscribers, and all those indebted to said estate are requested to make immediate payment (to prevent their accounts being put into an Attorney's hands), and enable us to make a dividend of his estate.
John Shaw, Hercules Mulligan   -   Administrators."

The John Grumly here referred to was Assistant Surrogate of New York County, and in the records of the Surrogate's court may be seen entries of wills, "proved before John Grumly, Esqr." at various dates in the year 1773. The "Colonial Land Papers" [1] also contain copies of a number of petitions in the years 1771 and 1772 by John Grumly and other citizens of New York, in relation to land grants in the vicinity of Lake George, showing that he was an extensive speculator in lands to be parcelled out under lease or sale to prospective settlers. The fact that the Surrogate entrusted Mulligan with the administration of the estate of so prominent a citizen indicates that he was a respected member of the community.

Some time between 1774 and 1776, Mulligan removed to Queen (now Pearl) Street. His business was that of a clothing merchant or general retailer of men's apparel, and his advertisements in the newspapers show that he employed a number of "taylors." From one of these advertisements we get an idea of the fashions of the day. Included in his stock were "'superfine cloths of the most fashionable colours"; "gold and silver lace, with some half laces for hats"; "gold and silver spangled buttons and loops"; "gold and silver treble French chain, gold and silver cord, tassels, vellum and threads"; "rich gold and silver spangled Brandenburgh"; "a large assortment of gold and silver fringe ornaments with bullion knots and epaulets"; "epaulets for gentlemen of the army and militia"; "Irish linnens," "gloves," "hat trimmings of all sorts," and "silk breeches and silks of all colours." Indeed, his stock was so large and so varied as to satisfy the most fastidious cravings of the dandies of the day, so we need not wonder at the family tradition that his establishment was fitted up "in elegant style." It was situated in what might be called the very pivot of the City's activities, and thus it became a sort of Mecca for the gay young "bloods" of the day, who came there to find out and discuss the fashions, on which subject it would seem Hercules Mulligan must have been something of an authority.

In fact, it seems to have been "quite the thing" for the grandees of the City to have their raiment made by the house of Mulligan, and people were known to make periodical trips to New York for that purpose from various parts of the Province. Indeed, he was honored with the patronage of no less distinguished a person than the first President of the United States, as is seen from the records and accounts kept by George Washington's private secretary, Colonel Tobias Lear. [2] During part of his first term as President, or from April, 1789, to October, 1790, Washington lived at No. 3 Cherry Street, New York, opposite Great George's (now Franklin) Square, a very short distance from Mulligan's shop at 23 Queen Street. His secretary had the handling of all monies for the President's household, and he maintained a comprehensive account of his daily expenditures, in which he entered not only every item disbursed but usually recorded its purpose. The amount, in each instance, is expressed in the English system of pounds, shillings and pence, for although the present decimal system of dollars and cents was adopted by Congress in 1787, it was not yet in general use. Colonel Lear's records contain the following entries covering Washington's dealings with Mulligan:

May 25, 1789—"By Contingent Exp.^{s} p.^{d} Mr. Hercules Mulligan for mak.^{g} a Surtout & a suit of clothes for the Presid.^{t} & cloth .... 25 9 9 "
July 23, 1789—"By Contingent Exp.^{s} p.^{d} Mr. Mulligan for a piece of Gingham bo.^{t} by him for Mrs. Washington .... 5 13 6 "
September 12, 1789—"By Contingent Exp.^{s} p.^{d} Hercules Mulligan for 6 yds. of flannel for Mrs Washington @ 14/—.............................. 4 4 0 "
September 28, 1789—"By Contingent & Ho. [house] Exp.^{s} p.^{d} Hercules Mulligan for two Acct.^{s} —one for 109-10-5 and one for 4-6-10½ .... 113 17 3½"
October 14, 1789—"By Conting.^{t} Exp.^{s} pd. Mr. H. Mulligan for 14½ yds. Velvet for a suit of clothes for the President @ 40/—............ 29 0 0 "
December 9, 1789—"By ditto. pd. Hercules Mulligan on acc.^{t} .... 80 0 0 "
May 5, 1790—"By Cont.^{gt} Exp.^{s} pd. H. Mulligan on acc.^{t} of Tayloring—part in advance.......... 30 0 0 "

These entries show that in less than a year Colonel Lear paid Mulligan on President Washington's account £228. 4s. 6½ d., for goods and services. The large item of September 28th, was for the President's clothes, and a suit of livery or a coat for one of his servants; the items of October 14th and December 9th included the cost of the clothes which the President wore at his weekly levees, and which a contemporary writer described as "a resplendent black velvet suit." These were extremely formal occasions, to which only "official characters and strangers of distinction" were invited, and since doubtless the President wished to appear at his best, he ordered this high-priced imported velvet and had the suit made by "one of the most fashionable merchant tailors of his day" [3] in New York.

As early as 1772, we find Hercules Mulligan on terms of intimate friendship with Alexander Hamilton. His brother, Hugh Mulligan, was a member of the importing house of Lawrence Kortright and Company of New York; and they were the owners of seven vessels engaged in the West Indian trade. [4] Lawrence Kortright, Jr., was the father-in-law of James Monroe, fifth President of the United States. [5] It was through this connection that Hercules formed a friendship with Hamilton, which was destined to continue, and did continue until the tragic end of that great statesman by a bullet from the pistol of Aaron Burr on July 12th, 1804.

When Hamilton came to America from his home in the Island of Nevis in the West Indies, in the year 1772, he brought letters of introduction "to certain agreeable and distinguished persons in New York. [6] We are told "he found lodgings with Hercules Mulligan, the fashionable clothier, whose brother was a junior partner in the importing firm of Kortright and Company, which acted as young Hamilton's bankers. Hamilton's West Indian patrons sent regular shipments of goods to this firm, which were credited to his account." [7] Another account of Alexander Hamilton states: "Hamilton arrived in Boston late in October (1772) and took passage immediately for New York. There had been no time to announce his coming, and he was obliged to find his own way to the house of Hercules Mulligan, a member of the West Indian firm, to whom Mr. Cruger [7a] had given him a warm letter of introduction. Mr. Mulligan, a good-natured Irishman, received him hospitably and asked him to stop in his modest house until his plans were made. Alexander accep-ted the invitation." [8] The statement that Hercules Mulligan was "a member of the West Indian firm," is an error, because we know that in 1772 Mulligan was in business for himself in Water Street. And Mulligan's own written statement says that the "warm letter of introduction" given by Mr. Cruger to Alexander Hamilton prior to his leaving home was addressed to the house of Kortright and Company, of which Hercules' brother, Hugh, was a member, and of which business he became the sole owner in the next year. [9]

Among the "Papers of Major-General Alexander Hamilton" at the Department of Manuscripts of the Library of Congress, there is a most interesting document entitled: "Narrative of Hercules Mulligan of the City of New York," a photographic reproduction of which is hereto annexed. The "Narrative" is undated, but in the opinion of the documentary experts at the Library of Congress, it was written "sometime between the years 1810 and 1815." Mulligan was then between seventy and seventy-five years of age, and in the natural course of events had not many more years of life before him. The Hamilton family were aware that he above all other citizens of New York was best acquainted with the events of Hamilton's early life in this country, and there is no doubt that Mulligan wrote the "Narrative" on the request of some member of the family, desirous of having an authentic record of the details before the aged man had passed away. In all likelihood, it was written on the request of John C. Hamilton, preparatory to his collection of the materials for his "Life" of his distinguished father, or about the year 1810.

As stated in the "Narrative of Hercules Mulligan," when Alexander Hamilton was a collegian and a resident of his (Mulligan's) house, he "used in the evenings to sit with my family and my brother's family and write doggerel rhymes for their amusement," and "was always amiable and cheerful and extremely attentive to his books." Doubtless, the politics of the day and the methods of solving the growing difficulties with England, which were then becoming the subject of universal interest in the Colonies, were discussed in the Mulligan household on those occasions, and in listening to the conversation of his host and his friends, young Hamilton obtained an insight into the aspirations and intentions of the patriots. In Mulligan's "Narrative" he said that he was "well acquainted" with Dr. Witherspoon, [10] president of Princeton College, and that he accompanied Hamilton to Princeton and "introduced Mr. Hamilton to him." That was in the year 1773.

It is remarkable to find the number of Irish Americans with whom Alexander Hamilton was associated. His first tutor was Dr. Hugh Knox, a native of

Armagh, Ireland, who came to America in the year 1753. [11] He first taught school in Delaware, but subsequently became a clergyman of the Presbyterian Church and removed to Saint Croix, where he established a school which Hamilton attended. Chief Justice Shea describes Dr. Knox as "a good, ripe scholar, of a frank and encouraging nature, of a graceful and unaffected elocution and of a mind susceptible to receive, and of a free disposition to impart to others, the influences of correct habits and religious sentiments." He adds: "Hamilton was most fortunate in having thus early the association and friendship of a person so cultivated and so religiously toned."

Among the letters which Hamilton brought from his West Indian home was one from Dr. Knox, introducing him to Dr. Francis Barber, master of an Academy at Elizabethtown, New Jersey, where Hamilton studied for one year. This Doctor Barber was a son of Patrick Barber, an immigrant from Longford, Ireland, to Orange County, N. Y., about 1735, [12] and who was one of the Judges of the Court of Common Pleas of Ulster County [13] in 1782. Hamilton's next meeting with Barber after leaving his school, was in 1776 when the latter was Lieutenant-Colonel of a regiment of the Continental army. In 1774, when Hamilton pursued the higher studies at King's College, [14] he studied medicine under the learned Doctors, Samuel Clossey [15] and James Magrath. Dr. Clossey is described by Dr. Allen McLane Hamilton [16] as "a clever Irish surgeon and a graduate of Trinity College, Dublin." He became Professor of Natural Philosophy on October 24th, 1765, and later Professor of Anatomy, at King's College, and in the *New York Journal or General Advertiser* of the year 1771 there are several announcements of Dr. Clossey's public lectures on "the Mechanics and Sciences," in which he signed himself "Fellow of the Royal College of Physicians in Dublin." James Magrath also was an Irishman. He had been a New York schoolmaster, [17] but became a physician, and the *New York Gazetteer* of April 14th, 1774, said of him that he was "a gentleman of great learning and a physician of the most exalted eminence."

Besides these Irishmen with whom Hamilton was early associated, we know that during the progress of the Revolutionary War, he was also on terms of close friendship with James Duane [18] and General John Sullivan , [19] and one of his notable literary efforts was a letter which he addressed to Duane in 1780, in which he made a remarkably able analysis of the defects of the Articles of Confederation, and the ideas conveyed in which were afterwards embodied to a large extent in the Constitution of the United States. It was Sullivan who proposed Hamilton to Washington in 1781 for the post of Secretary of the Treasury, and when in 1801, some prominent members of the Federalist Party, of which Hamilton was the leader, decided to establish a daily paper in New York (*The Evening Post*), its first editor, William Coleman, [20] was selected by Hamilton. Among Hamilton's intimate friends in Philadelphia were William Duane , [21] founder and editor of the Philadelphia *Aurora* (1794), and Thomas FitzSimons , [22] an eminent merchant of that

City. Hamilton bore witness to the help he received from FitzSimons in establishing the financial policy of the government and in funding the debt incurred in waging the Revolutionary War.

[1] Published by the Secretary of State; Albany, N. Y., 1864.
[2] Colonel Lear's original accounts are in the possession of the Decatur family. They were edited and published by Stephen Decatur, under the title of *Private Affairs of George Washington—from the Records and Accounts of Tobias Lear, Esquire, his Secretary;* Boston, Mass., 1933.
[3] Barrett's *Old Merchants of New York.*
[4] The *Narrative of Hercules Mulligan* shows that the firm was comprised of Lawrence Kortright and Hugh Mulligan. After the death of Kortright at Saint Croix in 1773, Hugh Mulligan continued the business alone in the firm name.
[5] James Monroe married Eliza, daughter of Lawrence Kortright on February 18, 1786.
[6] Morse, *Life of Alexander Hamilton.* See also Mulligan's "Narrative," appended hereto.
[7] *Alexander Hamilton,* by Johan J. Smertenko, p. 23; New York, 1932.
[7a] This was Nicholas Cruger, a merchant of New York and Saint Croix, in whose office at the latter place Hamilton had been employed for two years, and who at one time was president of the New York Chamber of Commerce.
[8] *The Conqueror, Being the True and Romantic Story of Alexander Hamilton,* by Gertrude Atherton, p. 118; New York, 1902.
[9] See "Narrative of Hercules Mulligan."
[10] Dr. John Witherspoon was president of Princeton from 1768 to 1794, and the only clergyman to sign the Declaration of Independence.
[11] Shea, *Life and Epoch of Alexander Hamilton;* Boston, 1880. See also The Conqueror, pp. 69-73.
[12] Eager, *History of Orange County,* N. Y.
[13] *New York Packet,* January 13, 1785.
[14] Subsequently named Columbia College.
[15] *The Conqueror,* p. 124.
[16] *Life of Alexander Hamilton.*
[17] His school was on Dock Street prior to 1750. He was a graduate of Trinity College, Dublin.
[18] Duane was a member of the Continental Congress and was the first Mayor of New York after the Revolution. He was a son of Anthony Duane of Cong, County Mayo, Ireland.
[19] Sullivan was a son of John Sullivan, who was born at Limerick, Ireland, in 1692. He was of the ancient Irish family of that name of the Counties of Kerry and Cork. He emigrated to America in 1723 and died at Durham, N. H., in 1796. He was a schoolmaster in Maine and New Hampshire for more than 60 years.
[20] Coleman was born in Boston of Irish parents in 1766.
[21] Duane came to this country from Clonmel, Co. Tipperary, Ireland.
[22] FitzSimons' birthplace in Ireland is unknown, though it is said that he was born in Limerick. He was an officer of the Revolutionary army. The mercantile house of which he was a member, George Meade and Company of Philadelphia, subscribed £1,000. to the support of the American troops in 1780.

Chapter Four

THE most authoritative accounts of Hamilton's early career are related by Chief Justice George Shea of the New York Marine Court and by John C. Hamilton, son of Alexander Hamilton. Chief Justice Shea, in referring to Hamilton's early life and school days, says: "He now qualified to enter upon a collegiate course. His preference was for Princeton and thither he went, accompanied by one who was, perhaps, his earliest friend in America, Mr. Hercules Mulligan. Mulligan was an Irishman. He was a brother of the junior member of the firm of Kortright and Company, to which firm produce was consigned from the West Indies to be sold and the proceeds applied to Hamilton's support. The amount was likely not more than sufficient for his simplest needs. When Hamilton came to reside in New York, it was at Mulligan's house that he made his home. Mulligan became very active soon after this time in the politics of the Revolution; was chosen by the citizens of New York a member of the Committee of One Hundred, and, after the battle of Long Island, while leaving New York he was captured on his way, brought back and detained in the City during the war. Now that we are speaking of this friend of Hamilton, it may as well be mentioned at once, that, when Hamilton received in 1777 his appointment to Washington's staff, Mulligan became a confidential correspondent of the Commander-in-Chief and furnished him most valuable intelligence. At the end of the war, when Washington had re-entered the City at the head of the American army, he showed his approbation and respect for Mr. Mulligan by taking his first breakfast there with him." [1]

This historic statement of Chief Justice Shea [2] is corroborated by the son of Alexander Hamilton, in his History of the Republic of the United States of America , as traced in the Writings of Alexander Hamilton. John C. Hamilton says: "Hercules Mulligan, from whose written narrative many of the incidents of Hamilton's early life are derived, was a brother of Mr. Mulligan of the firm of Kortright and Company, to whom West Indian produce was consigned, to be sold and appropriated to the support of Hamilton. He had been very active in the earlier scenes of the Revolution and out-lived most of the Revolutionary race. He was chosen one of the Committee of One Hundred and after the battle of Long Island, he, with many other Whigs, left the City. A party of Tories, it is related, seized him at midnight, threw a blanket over him and carried him to New York where he was detained. After Hamilton entered the family of Washington, Mulligan became the confidential correspondent of the Commander-in-Chief, furnished most important intelligence and apprised him of a plot to seize him. When Arnold reached New York Mulligan was seized and thrown into the Provost in hopes of fixing on him the evidence of having given information, but his skill was such that he was not detected. Upon the evacuation of that City, Washington complimented him by taking his first breakfast with this zealous patriot." [3]

Prior to the Revolution, there was a large Tory element in New York, [4] and the patriots complained bitterly of the tardiness of this City in aligning itself with the other colonies in open and effective rebellion and in uniting to form the first Congress. Public opinion was much divided, and in Force's *American Archives* may be read accounts of meetings of citizens in various parts of the Province as well as in other colonies, declaring their loyalty to the Crown and protesting against meetings and acts of the patriots, which were designed, they said, "to stir up bad blood." Great efforts were made by the latter to create enthusiasm for the cause of separation, but in some places without much success, the general idea among many of the people being that the colonies were too weak and England too powerful to hope for a successful outcome of an armed conflict. Indeed, it required much courage in some sections to declare oneself in favor of Independence or to express sentiments savoring of disloyalty to England.

When referring to this period, Chief Justice Shea gives an account of an indignation meeting held by citizens of New York in July, 1774, in "The Fields," [5] now City Hall Park, at which Alexander McDougall presided. "A great concourse of people" assembled here, and for a long time the gathering was called locally "the great meeting in The Fields." The Sons of Liberty, of whom Hercules Mulligan was a central figure, were the prime movers in organizing "the great meeting in The Fields," the object of which, according to Chief Justice Shea, "was to stir the half-hearted Assembly to some action and to urge upon it the meaning of heeding the voice of the patriots who were daily increasing in numbers."

Hamilton was then only eighteen years of age and Chief Justice Shea clearly intimates that the influence of his friend, Mulligan, had much to do with shaping the political opinions of the future American statesman, and that it was he who induced him to enroll in the Sons of Liberty. According to Shea, "Hamilton was among the auditors of this meeting and it would be unreasonable to suppose that Hercules Mulligan was not there also, perhaps with him. Hamilton was affiliated with the Sons of Liberty. His relations with William Livingston, John Mason, [6] John Rodgers [7] and particularly with his host, Hercules Mulligan, put him in frequent intercourse with those of that inclining." [8] It was at this meeting that the youthful Hamilton won his first laurels as a public speaker, and for which he has received in history well-deserved renown. His speech on that occasion, dealing with "British oppression" and "the duty of resistance," aroused his audience to a high pitch of excitement, and for several months thereafter he contributed articles to Holt's *Journal* on the controversy with England, which attracted wide attention.

Holt's *New York Journal or General Advertiser* of July 7th, and Rivington's *New York Gazetteer* of July 14th, 1774, published short reports of "the great meeting in The Fields." No account was given of the addresses except that of the chairman, who "explained the dangerous tendency of the numerous and vile arts used by the enemies of America to divide and distract her councils";

but the Resolutions, which "were passed without a dissentient," were printed in full. These Resolutions are couched in such language as to indicate plainly the temper of the people and that they were determined to have their grievances redressed, or that the connection with England be cast off entirely. They denounced as "oppressive" the Boston Port Act; declared that "any attempt to abridge the liberties of any one of the sister colonies is an attack upon the liberties of all the colonies"; they protested "against shutting up any of the ports of America"; that "all importation from and exportation to Great Britain be stopped, until Parliament repealed the Act blockading the port of Boston," and they called upon the Deputies who were to represent New York at the Congress to be held in Philadelphia in the following September, "to agree to non-importation from Great Britain until American grievances are redressed."

Thenceforward, colonial affairs became the subject of bitter controversies and a series of pamphlets was issued by both sides to the dispute, in which some of the ablest men of the day participated. We are told "the chief supporters of British despotism and supremacy were the Episcopal clergy, who derived their appointments and their livings from the Crown and who had been taught to regard the King as the supreme head of Church and State." [9] One of the most active among them was Rev. Samuel Seabury, pastor of St. Peter's Protestant Episcopal Church at Eastchester, Westchester County. On the Whig side of the dispute were arrayed such men as the Livingstons, Roosevelts, Jays, Ludlows, Lindley Murray, the celebrated grammarian, and others of that stamp, some of whom issued leaflets of great power and which had a wonderful effect in moulding public opinion. Rev. Seabury wrote several pamphlets pleading England's case, which were distributed widely by the royal authorities, not only in New York but through the neighboring Provinces. One of these, published in 1775 over the signature, "A Westchester Farmer," at once created a sensation. Alexander Hamilton, who had already written several political broadsides, replied to Seabury in a seventy-eight page pamphlet entitled "The Farmer Refuted, or a more Comprehensive and Impartial View of the Disputes between Great Britain and the Colonies," which was published on February 5, 1775, over the *nom-de-plume,* "A Sincere Friend of America." [10]

On this point, Hercules Mulligan wrote in his "Narrative": "While Mr. Hamilton was at College he wrote several Political essays, and in 1775 he wrote the 'Westchester Farmer Refuted' in my house and a part in my presence and read some of the pages to me as he wrote them. At the time this publication was attributed to Governor Livingston." After its appearance, Holt in his *New York Journal* called Hamilton "the Vindicator of Congress," and it was generally conceded that Hamilton had done more to hasten matters to a climax, by preparing the public mind for the Revolution that was to follow, than any other man in America.

Hamilton's pamphlet is a masterpiece of style, logical clearness and marshalling of facts and gives a splendid insight to New York politics of pre-Revolutionary days. Its appearance became the talk of the country, and as its author was unknown, it was attributed by some to Governor Livingston and by others to John Jay, on account of the great fame of those distinguished men. But, Dr. Smucker says that "when it was hinted to Dr. Cooper, President of King's College, that Alexander Hamilton, a youth of eighteen, was suspected by some to have written it, he treated the suggestion as absurd in the extreme." [11] "Nevertheless," says Dr. Smucker, "the truth came out at last and it was proven by Messrs. Troup [12] and Mulligan, two associates of Hamilton, that he alone was the author." [13]

Dr. Smucker's statement is corroborated by Chief Justice Shea, who, in referring to Hamilton's famous pamphlet, says: "When a lad of nineteen was discovered to be the author, incredulity was surely pardonable. The collegian who had spoken to 'the meeting in the Fields' a few months before was publicly disclosed to have been the author. Hercules Mulligan was not the man to keep it a secret, nor to allow his young and gifted lodger to remain in the shade, for Hamilton had read the manuscript to him in his room at the residence in Water Street." [14] This indicates clearly that Hamilton placed much confidence in his friend Mulligan, and that the latter must have been a man of some education, and, in Hamilton's opinion, of good judgment and foresight. Why the historians of the Revolution failed to mention the part he played in those stirring times is difficult to understand. [15]

How important was Mulligan's influence over Alexander Hamilton at this time may be judged from the fact that "Hamilton had grown up with a deep reverence for the British Constitution and his strong aristocratic prejudices inclined him to all the aloofness of the true conservative." [16] It was a very serious matter in those days for one to exhibit anti-English feelings in America, for the government officials were constantly on the alert for all such manifestations, and in New York especially, "the soldiers swaggered around the streets with a sharp eye for aggression." Hamilton had been reared in an atmosphere of pro-English sentiment, and his biographers all agree that the question as to which side he would take in the coming conflict was discussed freely among his friends. "In the beginning," says Renwick, "he showed predilections toward England and his sympathies were all with England." Elbert Hubbard also informs us that "at his boarding house and at school he argued the question hotly, defending England's right to tax her dependencies," and on being asked on one occasion, "in case of war, on which side will you fight, Hamilton answered: *on the side of England.'" Hubbard then speaks of "the young man's conversion" and how "next morning he announced at the boarding house that he believed the Colonies were right." [17]

Hubbard does not mention the names of those "at his boarding house" with whom Hamilton "argued the question hotly," but, may we not properly assume that the enthusiastic Irishman in whose home he lived found some moments of delight in entering into the discussion, and that he took particular pains to convince his young friend of "the error of his ways"? And may we not also be permitted to picture to ourselves a scene at the breakfast-table in the Mulligan household on the "next morning," when Hamilton, after ruminating over the arguments of his host, confessed his belief that "the Colonies were right"? Indeed, according to one of Hamilton's biographers: "Hercules Mulligan, possessed of the traditional Irish hatred of the English, was an early and ardent patriot; his arguments with the loyal West Indian (Alexander Hamilton) were many; his influence on the young philosopher's thoughts considerable; and his contribution to Hamilton's earliest reputation with the ladies, in the form of fashionable doublets and smallclothes, were most welcome to a proud heart and a lean purse." [18]

On the 22nd of November, 1774, another meeting of the citizens assembled at the City Hall, where a Committee of sixty persons, "chosen from the Freeholders and Freemen of the City," was elected. This was the first "Committee of Observation." We are told that the members were "chosen without a dissenting voice," and the full membership, as it appeared in Rivington's New York Gazeteer of November 24th, 1774, will be found below. [19] Here again we find the Irish patriot, Hercules Mulligan, honored by association with eminent Americans of the day.

[1] Shea, *The Life and Epoch of Alexander Hamilton;* pp. 173-174.
[2] See also the interesting reference to Hercules Mulligan, at page 85, by no less an authority than Washington's adopted son, George Washington Parke Custis.
[3] *History of the Republic of the United States of America, as traced in the Writings of Alexander Hamilton;* Vol. i, p. 46; Phila., 1864. See also *The Life of Alexander Hamilton,* by John C. Hamilton; Vol. 1, pp. 8-9.
[4] Mrs. Atherton states in *The Conqueror,* p. 128, that New York at this time was "the hot-bed of Toryism," and Professor Flick, in Loyalism in New York, estimates that "at least 15,000 New York loyalists joined the British army and 8,500 the navy."
[5] "The Fields" were also known as "The Common." At that time it was a woodland; giant sycamore, maple and walnut trees and numerous weeping-willows occupied the space now covered by the City Hall Park, and according to published accounts, when the City Hall was erected some years later, "the trees were cut down in order to favor the populace with an improved view of the architectural front of the great marble edifice."
[6] Dr. Mason was then Pastor of the Presbyterian Church in Cedar Street between Nassau Street and Broadway.
[7] This was Dr. John Rodgers, also a Presbyterian clergyman.
[8] Shea, *Life and Epoch of Alexander Hamilton;* p. 279.
[9] *Life and Times of Alexander Hamilton,* by Dr. Samuel M. Smucker; Boston, 1857.
[10] A copy of this pamphlet may be seen among "The Official and other Papers of the late Major-General Alexander Hamilton, compiled from the originals in the possession of Mrs. Hamilton," which were published in New York under that title in the year 1842.

[11] Mrs. Atherton, in referring to the pamphlets of which Hamilton was the author, relates an amusing incident of their reception by the loyal Dr. Cooper. She says: "It was not long before the public had the author's name. Troup had been present at the writing of the pamphlets and he called on Dr. Cooper one day and announced the authorship with considerable gusto.

"'I'll not believe it,' exclaimed the president, angrily, 'Mr. Jay wrote those pamphlets, and none other. A mere boy like that; it's absurd. Why do you bring me such a story, sir? I don't like this Hamilton, he's too forward and independent, but I have no desire to hear more of him.'

"'He wrote them, sir, and Mulligan, in whose house he lives, and I can prove it. He's the finest brain in this country and I mean you shall know it.'

"He left Dr. Cooper foaming, and went to spread the news elsewhere. The effect of his revelation was immediate distinction for Hamilton." (*The Conqueror;* p. 137.)

[12] This was Robert Troup, a lawyer and one of Hamilton's most intimate friends, who after the Revolution, became United States Judge for the District of New York.

[13] Smucker, *Life and Times of Alexander Hamilton;* p. 34.

[14] Shea, *Life and Epoch of Alexander Hamilton;* p. 257. See also Mulligan's "Narrative."

[15] There are numerous instances of historical works wherein Mulligan's countrymen were similarly ignored. For example, in a book entitled *New York City During the War of the Revolution,* bearing the approval of a professor of history at Columbia University, there is not the slightest mention of Hercules Mulligan. And of his contemporaries in New York, the only Irishmen to whom the author refers were Hugh Gaine, Hugh Wallace and Dennis Ryan. Yet, in the Revolutionary period there were many other Irishmen prominent in the business and social affairs of the City, notably such men as Daniel McCormick, John and William Leary, Christopher Colles, Dominick Lynch, William Mooney, John and William Kelly, Samuel Loudon, Alexander McComb and Patrick Walsh. And in his chapter on the City's teachers, the author of this book could find no space for Dr. Samuel Clossey or Clohissey, under whom Alexander Hamilton studied medicine, for Dr. James Magrath, educator, lecturer and physician, or for any of the Irish schoolmasters who taught New York youth in the days of the Revolution!

[16] *The Conqueror;* p. 128.

[17] Elbert Hubbard, *Little Journeys to the Homes of American Statesmen;* p. 83, New York, 1898.

[18] *Alexander Hamilton,* by Johan J. Smertenko; p. 23, New York, 1932.

[19] From Rivington's *New York Gazeteer* of November 24, 1774:

"Tuesday, November 22, 1774.

The election of a Committee of sixty persons for the purposes mentioned in the Association entered into by the Congress, having this day come on, pursuant to advertisements in the public news-papers; a respectable number of the Freeholders and Freemen of this City assembled at the City-Hall where the election was conducted under the inspection of several of the Vestrymen. And the following persons were chosen without a dissenting voice, viz:

COMMITTEE OF OBSERVATION

Isaac Low
Henry Remsen
Robert Benson
Philip Livingston
Peter T. Curtenius
William W. Gilbert
James Duane
Abraham Brasher
John Berrian
John Alsop
Abraham P. Lott
Gabriel W. Ludlow
John Jay
Abraham Duryee
Nicholas Roosevelt
Peter Van Brugh Livingston
Joseph Bull
Edward Flemming
Isaac Sears
Francis Lewis
Lawrence Embree
David Johnston
John Lasher
Samuel Jones
Charles Nicoll
John Roome
John De Lancey
Alexander McDougall
Joseph Totten
Frederick Jay
Thomas Randall
Thomas Ivers
William W. Ludlow
Leonard Lispenard
HERCULES MULLIGAN
John B. Moore
Edward Laight
John Anthony
George Janeway
William Walton
William Goforth
Rudolphus Ritzeman
John Broome
William Denning
Lindley Murray
Joseph Hallett
Isaac Roosevelt
Lancaster Burling
Charles Shaw
Jacob Van Voorhees
Francis Basset
Nicholas Hoffman
Jeremiah Platt
Victor Bicker
Abraham Walton
William Ustick
John White
Peter Van Schaack
Comfort Sands
Theophilus Anthony"

Chapter Five

THE influential place occupied by Hercules Mulligan among the citizens of New York at this time, and the qualifications which enabled him to sustain with success a position in public affairs, are illustrated in other ways. The famous "Non-Importation Agreement," which was also known as "The Association of 1774," was formulated at a meeting of the Continental Congress on October 6th, 1774. In paragraph one of the articles of association it was declared: "that from and after the first day of December next, we will not import into British America from Great Britain or Ireland any goods, wares, or merchandise whatever," etc. In paragraph ten, it was agreed "that in case any merchant, trader or other person, shall import any goods or merchandise, after the first day of December, or before the first day of February next, the same ought forthwith, at the election of the owner, to be either reshipped or be delivered up to the Committee of the County or Town wherein they shall be imported, to be stored at the risque of the importer, until the non-importation agreement shall cease, or be sold under the direction of the Committee aforesaid." And it was further directed "that a Committee be chosen in every county, city or town, by those who are qualified to vote for representatives in the legislature, whose business it shall be attentively to observe the conduct of all persons touching this association; and when it shall be made to appear, to the satisfaction of a majority of any such committee, that any person within the limits of their appointment has violated this Association, that such majority do forthwith cause the truth of the case to be published in the gazette, to the end that all such foes of the rights of British-America may be publickly known and universally contemned as the enemies of American liberty, and thence forth we respectively will break off all dealings with him or her." [1] This document was signed by fifty-two members of the Continental Congress at Philadelphia on October 29th, 1774, and among its signers were John Sullivan, James Duane, Thomas McKean, Thomas Lynch, George Read and John and Edward Rutledge, all sons of Irish immigrants, while part of the original document is in the handwriting of Charles Thomson, Secretary of the Congress, who was a native of Ireland.

In accordance with the Non-Importation Agreement, the New York Committee of Observation took the matter in charge and notified the merchants of the City, and in the newspapers of the day may be seen a number of advertisements by New York merchants declaring their desire "to comply with the Association entered into by the late Continental Congress." A subcommittee of six was appointed to carry out the orders of Congress, and among the number we find Hercules Mulligan. The following advertisement appeared in the *New York Journal or General Advertiser* of December 22nd, 1774: "The subscribers have imported in the brig, *Elliott,* John Pym, from Liverpool, which sailed from thence the 28th, July last, and arrived here the 17th instant, the following goods." It then gave a long description of the cargo of the *Elliott,* appended to which was a statement in these words: "And we being desirous to comply with the association entered into by the Late Continental Congress, give this public notice that the above goods will be sold at Captain Doran's [2] [3] on Friday morning, the 23rd, instant, under the directions of the Committee." Then followed the names of the importers who signed the declaration and an announcement reading: "For particulars apply to John De Lancey, John Anthony, Joseph Totten, Hercules Mulligan, Victor Becker and Henry Remsen, the Sub-Committee."

The activities of the patriots throughout the winter of 1774 greatly strengthened the war feeling and on the first of March, 1775, the Committee of Observation called on the inhabitants to attend a meeting to be held at "The Exchange" on the evening of March 6th, for the purpose of selecting delegates to the then ensuing Congress. The loyalists determined to contest the election, and on the 3rd of March they assembled at La Montagnie's tavern, and resolved to attend the meeting of the 6th and oppose the action of the patriots. To meet this emergency, a number of the "Liberty Boys" met secretly on the following evening at the tavern of Daniel Sullivan [4] in "The Common" and there laid plans to resist the loyalists in whatever action they would take.

On the 6th of March the loyalists met in great force in "The Common" and marched to "The Exchange," amid the jeers of the patriots. The latter immediately divided themselves into three separate bodies, and headed by Captain Isaac Sears, Richard Livingston and Hercules Mulligan, each marched through different sections of the City with fifes and drums playing, and when they had collected all the men and boys that could be mustered they met at an agreed point, and thence, amid wild excitement, the entire assemblage marched to the place of the election. As spokesman for the patriots, Sears demanded "that a vote be taken by all the citizens present" and he threatened violence to anyone who would insist upon the election on any other ground. The loyalists demanded "a vote on the official poll only," but the Committee refused, and a majority of those present having signified that they favored the popular nominees, the Committee declared them elected and the meeting broke up in confusion. Sears, Livingston and Mulligan became the heroes of the hour. This was the first time that the loyalists had come together in such large numbers in public meeting and the republicans had an opportunity of observing their strength, and then and there the gage of battle was thrown down between the opposing parties, and the leading loyalists became marked men.

Captain Sears was known popularly as "King Sears," and for sometime after the incident just related he was engaged in drilling the youth of the City, who sympathized with the patriot cause. He received active cooperation from Mulligan, who went about quietly organizing for the Sons of Liberty, and on one occasion in the Summer of 1775, we find these two uncompromising patriots engaged in another daring enterprise. The City Corporation had stored a quantity of muskets in the armory, and Sears conceived the idea of seizing the arms. By the aid of a friendly watchman, the raid was carried out successfully and in due time the muskets were distributed among the "Liberty Boys," and thereafter Sears and his men made nightly visits to the houses of certain Tories who were known or were suspected to have arms in their possession. In November of the same year, Sears headed a troop of horsemen from Connecticut, who raided the office of Rivington's Royal Gazette, moved the printing presses to New Haven and melted the types into bullets. This act of the redoubtable Sears, like the destruction of the statue of the King in the next year, in which he also took part, created great consternation among the Tories.

We learn from authentic history that when the news of the battle of Lexington reached New York, the City was precipitated almost instantly into a state of the most alarming confusion, and one of the first acts of the patriots was to hold a meeting in "The Common," at which the majority demanded "the shutting up of the port immediately," and with that purpose a number of the members of the "Committee of Secrecy and Inspection" called on Andrew Elliott, Collector of the Port, and "demanded the keys of the Custom House." [5] Within a few days, a committee of "one hundred men of eminence" [6] was chosen to direct the affairs of the City until a Congress of the people could be elected. A "Call for a Provincial Congress by the Citizens of New York" was issued on April 26th, 1775, and a copy of this document in the "Calendar of Historical Manuscripts relating to the War of the Revolution," [7] now in the office of the Secretary of State, shows that Hercules Mulligan was one of its signers. [8]

Five days after the issuance of this "Call," or on May 1st, 1775, the "General Committee of the City of New York," or "Committee of One Hundred" as it was generally called, [9] was formed for the purpose of taking over the government of the City. And in further evidence of the esteem in which the Irish patriot was held by his fellow citizens, the name of Hercules Mulligan is found on the roster of this historic committee. [10] A complete list of its members will be found below, [11] and as the New York historian, James Grant Wilson, says, "they were the leading patriots of the City." The membership of this committee was chosen with the greatest care and discrimination, for not until the names proposed had been canvassed by the patriots over and over again, and they had insisted upon the elimination of certain men whose lukewarmness in the cause they had some reason to suspect, was the list acceptable to all. [12] On November 22nd, 1775, Mulligan was also chosen one of the Revolutionary Committee of Correspondence, as well of a new Committee of Observation. [13] These bodies usually met at Fraunces' Tavern and sometimes at the City Hall, which then stood where the United States Sub-Treasury is now, at Wall and Nassau Streets.

In Holt's *New York Journal or General Advertiser* of the years 1775 and 1776 there are several accounts of the meetings of these Revolutionary Committees, and in Force's American Archives [14] may also be seen copies of the entries in the "Journal of the Proceedings of the General Committee of the City of New York." All issues of the New York newspapers of this period are not now available, but the published reports [15] of twelve meetings of the General Committee in 1775 and 1776 show that Hercules Mulligan was recorded as present at ten. According to the newspaper accounts, as well as those published in Force's American Archives, the average attendance at these twelve meetings was only thirty-seven, and as Mulligan is on record as attending over eighty percent of the meetings, we can readily see that he was an enthusiastic patriot and that he entered into the serious business of this Committee with alacrity and determination. At one of its meetings held at "The Exchange" on July 5th, 1775, it was "Ordered that William W. Ludlow, Hercules Mulligan, Oliver Templeton [16] and Anthony Van Dam be added to the Committee of Inspection and that the names of the said Committee be published under the Resolves of this day and in handbills to be given to the Pilots." [17] The full title of this body was the "Committee of Secrecy and Inspection." It was comprised of seventeen members, [18] whose names will be found below. [19]

There is also recorded a meeting of New York merchants, held on July ioth, 1775, when an association was formed "for the purpose of giving circulation to Bills of Credit of Connecticut." On this occasion nearly two hundred New York merchants signed a declaration to this effect: "We the subscribers sensible of the advantages to be derived from the trade of the province of Connecticut, and desirous of giving their Bills of Credit a currency equal to those of the other neighbouring Colonies, do promise and oblige ourselves to receive the same in all payments whatsoever." One of the signers to this agreement was Hercules Mulligan, [20] and it is also of interest to note that Dennis McReady, Oliver Templeton, Thomas Dougherty, Jr., Daniel McCormick, Hugh Gaine and Patrick McDavitt, all except Dougherty natives of Ireland, were among the signers. [21] The New York General Committee on the next day, July nth, passed a resolution recommending to the inhabitants "to take the paper Bills of Credit of Connecticut in payments and to give it the same degree of circulation and credit as is now given to the Bills of Credit of the neighbouring Colonies." This resolution was printed and distributed among the citizens and was signed by Henry Remsen, Deputy Chairman.

[1] *Journals of the Continental Congress;* Vol. i, pp. 75-81, reprint by Govt. Ptg. Office, Washington, 1904.
[2] This was Thomas Doran, merchant and sea-captain, at whose house "The Marine Society of New York City" used to hold its meetings. See Gaine's *New York Gazette and Weekly Mercury* of April 4, 1771, also Rivington's *New York Gazetteer* of July 8, 1773. Gaine's paper throughout 1777 and 1778, contained announcements of "the Quarterly Meetings of the Marine Society at the house of the Widow Doran, near the Old Slip."
[3] In the "Calendar of Historical Manuscripts of the Province and State of New York," transcribed from the original records by Edmund B. O'Callaghan, and published by authority of the Legislature, appears a petition dated January 3, 1757, by Lawrence Kortright, partner of Hugh Mulligan, "for a commission to Captain Thomas Doran as commander of the sloop *Harlequin*."
[4] The tavern of Daniel Sullivan was known as "The Bunch of Grapes" and was a popular meeting place for the "Liberty Boys." It stood on what is now the block occupied by the Potter Building and the old *Times* building in City Hall Square.
[5] "Letters of Thomas Ellison, Jr., of New York in 1775, to his father. Col. Thomas Ellison of New Windsor, New York," in *Magazine of American History;* Vol. VIII, pp. 279-286.
[6] Mrs. Martha J. Lamb, in *Magazine of American History.*
[7] These historical manuscripts were compiled by the Secretary of State and were published by order of the Legislature, and a copy of the "Call" here referred to may be seen at page 4, volume 1, of these collections.
[8] SIGNERS TO THE CALL FOR A PROVINCIAL CONGRESS, April 26th, 1775:

Isaac Low	Philip Livingston	James Duane
Alexander McDougall	William Walton	John Broome
Victor Bicker	John White	Theophilus Anthony

John Alsop	William Denning	HERCULES MULLIGAN
Joseph Hallett	Abraham Brasher	Thomas Ivers
William Goforth	John Berrien	Frederick Jay
Abraham P. Lott	Isaac Roosevelt	Peter V. B. Livingston
Abraham Walton	Francis Lewis	John Anthony
Jeremiah Platt	Nicholas Roosevelt	George Janeway
Abraham Duryee	Jacob Van Voorhees	William W. Ludlow
Henry Remsen	John Lasher	Rudolphus Ritzeman
Robert Platt	Edward Fleming	Lancaster Burling
Joseph Bull	John Jay	David Johnston
Peter T. Curtenius	Joseph Totten	Francis Bassett
Robert Benson	John De Lancey	

[9] It was sometimes called the "Provisional War Committee" and also the "Committee of Resistance."

[10] See *Documents relating to the Colonial History of the State of New York;* Vol. VIII, p. 601, published under an Act of the Legislature by John Romeyn Broadhead and edited by Dr. E. B. O'Callaghan, Albany, 1857. It is stated here that the original list of the members of the Committee is at the State Paper office of the Privy Council at the British Museum, document number CLXVII.

[11] "GENERAL COMMITTEE, or COMMITTEE OF ONE HUNDRED, New York, May 1st, 1775. This day the following Gentlemen were chosen a General Committee for the City and County of New York in the present alarming crisis":

Isaac Low	David Johnston	Nicholas Hoffman
Lindley Murray	Thomas Smith	John Reade
Jeremiah Platt	Lawrence Embree	William Seton
Philip Livingston	Alexander McDougall	Abraham Walton
Lancaster Burling	James Desbrosses	John Van Cortlandt
Jacob Van Voorhees	Samuel Jones	Evert Bancker
James Duane	Thomas Randall	Peter W. Van Schaack
John Lasher	Augustus Van Horne	Jacobus Van Zandt
Comfort Sands	John De Lancey	Robert Bay
John Alsop	Leonard Lispenard	Henry Remsen
George Jane way	Garret Keteltas	Gerardus Duyckinck
Robert Benson	Frederick Jay	Nicholas Bogert
John Jay	William Walton	Peter T. Curtenius
James Beekman	Eleazar Miller	Peter Goelet
John Berrien	William W. Ludlow	William Laight
Peter V. B. Livingston	John Broome	Abraham Brasher
Samuel Verplanck	Benjamin Kissam	John Marston
William W. Gilbert	John White	Samuel Broome
Isaac Sears	Joseph Hallet	Abraham P. Lott
Richard Yates	John Morin Scott	Thomas Marston
Nicholas Roosevelt	Walter Franklin	John Lamb
HERCULES MULLIGAN	Gabriel W. Ludlow	Abraham Duryee
David Clarkson	Cornelius Clopper	John Morton
Edwin Fleming	David Beekman	Daniel Phoenix

Joseph Bull	Thomas Ivers	Victor Bicker
George Folliot	Hamilton Young	William Goforth
Daniel Dunscomb	Oliver Templeton	Thomas Buchanan
Francis Lewis	John Anthony	John B. Moore
Jacobus Lefferts	Abraham Brinkerhoff	William Denning
Anthony Van Dam	Lewis Pintard	Petrus Byvanck
Joseph Totten	Francis Bassett	Rudolphus Ritzeman
Richard Sharp	Theophilus Anthony	Isaac Roosevelt
John Imlay	Cornelius P. Low	Benjamin Helme

[12] Notwithstanding this, some of the members of the committee, after hostilities had actually begun, became loyalists and the names of twelve of its members may be found as signatories to a loyal address to Sir William Howe in October, 1776 (see copy of the address in *New York City During The Revolution*, published by the Mercantile Library Association, N. Y., 1861). The Chairman of the Committee was Isaac Low, but he afterwards sided with the Tories, according to an announcement in the *New York Journal or General Advertiser* of November 29, 1779, which on that date published the names of 58 persons whose "estates were declared forfeited for their adherence to the enemies of the State."
[13] *History of the City of New York*, by James Grant Wilson; Vol. II, p. 441.
[14] 4th Series, Vols. 2 and 4.
[15] In Holt's paper.
[16] Oliver Templeton was an Irishman and was a member of the Society of the Friendly Sons of Saint Patrick in 1784 (see *Early Celebrations of Saint "Patrick's Day*, by John D. Crimmins; p. 430). He was a merchant, and a number of his advertisements may be seen in New York newspapers as early as 1764.
[17] *American Archives;* 4th Ser., Vol. 11, p. 1375.
[18] Patrick Dennis was added to the Committee on October 3, 1773 (*American Archives;* 4th Ser., Vol. n, p. 940). He also was an Irishman and a patriot of the Revolution. He was Lieutenant of the Second Company of Artillery raised in New York in 1775 and later a Captain. Captain Dennis was the man who put down the obstructions in the East River after the capture of Long Island in August 1776, to prevent navigation by English warships and on November 6, 1776, the Committee of Safety ordered that "£500 be paid him on account moneys due him on that account." In the following month he was in charge of the building of boats at Poughkeepsie for the use of the American army (*Journal of the New York Committee of Safety;* Vol. I, pp. 705 and 730; Albany, 1842).
[19] Committee of Secrecy and Inspection:

John Imlay	Abraham P. Lott	William Bedlow
John Berrian	Cornelius Clopper	William Denning
Thomas Buchanan	Oliver Templeton	John Woodward
William Goforth	Evert Bancker	William W. Ludlow
Joseph Bull	Daniel Phoenix	Garret Kettletas
Anthony Van Dam	Hercules Mulligan	

[20] Force's *American Archives;* 4th Ser., Vol. II, p. 1622.
[21] Ibid.

Chapter Six

In 1776, before New York fell into possession of the enemy, a large number of the inhabitants were seized and accused of being involved in a conspiracy against the patriots. The situation received the serious attention of the Provincial Congress, and at one of their meetings one Joseph Smith testified to his having heard a conversation between some Tory patrons of the "Sergeants-Arms" tavern, "concerning a conspiracy on foot to seize some of the principal persons in the army of the American States." Thereupon, the Congress ordered the arrest of Gilbert Forbes, one of the leading Tories, and the seizure of his letters and papers, and we find the following entry in the record of the committee of enquiry:

"The Provincial Congress having taken the above letters into consideration, and finding from other circumstances that a most wicked and dangerous conspiracy was formed against the liberties of America, judged proper to appoint a committee of enquiry, with powers to examine into the nature of it and to sit in judgment in bringing to condign punishment such person or persons as they should find concerned in it. The following persons were appointed a Committee for the purpose

President, Peter R. Livingston
J. M. Scott
John Abeel
Marinus Willett
Corn. Byvanck
Alex McDougall
John Berrien
Herc. Mulligan
Gershom Mott
Peter Curtenius
John Stoutenburgh
James Wessels
John Crimshire
Gilbert Smith, Secretary"

The records of this committee were seized and taken to England after the war, and were published in London in 1786, under the title of "Minutes of the Trial and Examination of Certain Persons in the Province of New York, charged with being engaged in a Conspiracy against the Authority of the Congress and the Liberties of America." From these Minutes we obtain further insight into the sturdy character of Hercules Mulligan. The initial meeting of the committee was held on June 23, 1776, and Forbes was the first of the conspirators brought to trial. After the accusation and certain incriminating papers found on the prisoner were read by the presiding officer, Forbes addressed the committee, denying all knowledge of or connection with the alleged conspiracy, and it is evident that Hercules Mulligan could not restrain his indignation, for he rose immediately and said: "Sir! Sir! I am surprised you have the boldness to speak in this manner before the Committee, after what you have been guilty of. We do not sit here to hear you criminate, neither will such language avail you. Sir, we have authentic evidence of your having been concerned in a hellish conspiracy, and we are informed that you were desirous of obtaining mercy, by making an honest and full confession; as a friend, I advise you to conceal nothing, as you hope for pardon." [1]

From all of this we see that Hercules Mulligan was a man of considerable importance in the community and that his fellow-citizens recognized his worth and had the utmost confidence in his patriotism. Doubtless, his Celtic enthusiasm frequently brought him into contact with the leading patriots of the day, and Irish-like, he revelled in the opportunity to take part in the anti-English agitation then hourly growing in volume and intensity. As a member of these committees, he was in illustrious company, as may be seen from the names of his associates, some of them the most conspicuous in the Revolutionary history of the City of New York. Among them are noted Philip Livingston, a signer of the Declaration of Independence; his brother, Peter Van Brugh Livingston, Treasurer of the New York Revolutionary Congress; John Jay, who became the first Chief Justice of the United States, Secretary for Foreign Affairs and United States Minister to Spain; James Duane, member of the Continental Congress and who would have been a signer of the Declaration of Independence but for an accident which prevented his arrival at Philadelphia; and a number of others closely identified with the early history of New York in its mercantile, banking, legal, political and social affairs, and not less than twenty of whom are today commemorated in the street names of the City. John Morin Scott, James Duane, Benjamin Kissam, William Walton, Lindley Murray and Robert Benson constitute an array of names famous among the legal lights of early New York; George Folliot, John Imlay, Henry Remsen, Samuel Verplanck, John Alsop, Lewis Pintard, Jacobus Van Zandt, Anthony Van Dam and Oliver Templeton were the "merchant princes" of their time; Walter Franklin was reputed to be "the richest man in New York"; Thomas Randall was a shipowner and sea captain; Abraham P. Lott and Peter T. Curtenius were New York Aldermen; Daniel Phoenix, Isaac Roosevelt and Gulian Verplanck were financiers, and among the leading society men in the City were Gabriel H. Ludlow, John Reade, Daniel Clarkson, the Marstons and others whose names appear on these Revolutionary Committees. Were any proof wanting to illustrate the standing of Hercules Mulligan, we need look no further than the fact that he was associated with such eminent citizens, and by their choice of him as a member of such important committees it is evident that he was entrusted with the secrets and aspirations of the patriots.

There is no mention of Hercules Mulligan in the Revolutionary records, as far as I can find, except those herein alluded to. It is quite evident he did not enlist in any military body; but, that is not surprising, for there are also missing from the army rolls the names of many well-known patriots of the Revolution. It cannot be said, however, that he was entirely inactive in the military sense, for in 1775 he took part in the organization of a military company. The New York Provincial Congress, at a meeting on August 22nd, 1775, directed "that every County, City, Manor, Town and Precinct within this Colony be divided into Districts or Beats by the respective Committees, in such Manner that out of each may be formed one Military Company, ordinarily to consist of about Eighty-Three able-bodied and effective Men, Officers included, between Fifteen and Fifty years of age." And the Congress further directed, "That two Committee-Men at Least attend in each District or Beat for the Purpose of choosing the above-mentioned, who shall be Persons who have signed the general Association recommended by Congress." In conformance to this order, the City of New York was divided into twenty-four "Districts or Beats." District number fourteen comprised the section bounded by William, George, Chatham and Queen Streets, and Victor Bicker and Hercules Mulligan were the Committeemen in charge of that District, and raised the required quota of men. [2]

This was not the only military company in whose organization Mulligan took part. During the winter of 1775, before any steps were taken in New York to organize a regular force of artillery, Alexander Hamilton took instructions in gunnery from a British bombardier. Thus prepared, he applied for the command of a company of artillery ordered to be raised by the Committee of Safety, and on the 14th of March, 1776, he was appointed "'Captain of the Provincial Company of Artillery," but "on the condition (relates Mulligan in his "Narrative"), that he should raise Thirty Men." The company was recruited in the following July, and as the "Narrative" states, Mulligan cooperated with his friend, Hamilton, in raising the number of men required by the regulations of the Committee of Safety.

In the "Narrative of Hercules Mulligan" will be noted a reference to his having been "engaged in hauling off one of the cannon," which were mounted on the Battery prior to the 23rd of August, 1775, and according to all accounts, this was one of the most thrilling incidents of the early days of the Revolution in the City of New York. On the Battery seawall at this time there were twenty-one pieces of artillery under the command of Captain John Lamb. The conflict had not yet reached New York, but there were anchored in the harbor several British warships with a large force of soldiers and marines, and as they were in a position at any moment to seize the cannon, the Provincial Congress ordered Captain Lamb to remove the guns to the fortifications in the Highlands of the Hudson. Game's paper of August 28th, 1775, gave the following account of this incident:

"The Provincial Congress having resolved that the Cannon should be removed from the Battery, a Number of Citizens collected for that Purpose last Wednesday Evening, and Part of the Provincial Artillery under the Command of Captain John Lamb were posted on the Battery to prevent the Landing of any Party from the Asia Man of War, to annoy them while at work. When they marched down, which was about 11 o'clock, they observed one of the above Ship's Barges lying at some Distance from the Shore, where she continued upwards of an Hour; then she got under Sail and fired a Musket at the Men that were posted on the Battery. This was immediately returned by a smart Fire of Musketry from the Artillery and a few of the Independent Light-Infantry, belonging to Colonel Lasher's Battalion, that were likewise posted there for the above purpose. Soon after this, the *Asia* fired three Cannon, when our Drums beat to Arms, which alarmed the Inhabitants; when they had assembled she began a heavy and smart Fire of Nine, Eighteen and Twenty-four Pounders, and some Grapeshot; succeeded by a Discharge of Musketry from the Marines, but without doing any other Mischief than damaging the upper Part of several Houses near the Fort and White-Hall and wounding three Men. Notwithstanding the Fire from the *Asia*, the Citizens effected their purpose and carried off twenty-one Pieces of Cannon, being all that were mounted on Carriages. Since this Disturbance the Women and Children have been continually moving out of Town with their most valuable Effects."

The shot from the *Asia* was the opening of hostilities on the City of New York, and the fact that Hercules Mulligan was there as a participant in the daring enterprise of "hauling off the cannon" shows that he was fearless of the consequences and was ready to do a man's part in defense of the City.

A story has also come down in the family that on the evening of July 9th, 1776, after the Declaration of Independence was read to the Continental troops in "The Common," in the presence of Washington and his staff, Hercules Mulligan and the noted Revolutionary character, Isaac Sears, were among the leaders of that impetuous band of patriots who suddenly left the assemblage, rushed down "The Broad-Way" to Bowling Green, and tore down the leaden statue of the English King. The *New York Gazette and Weekly Mercury* of July 15, 1776, in its account of the destruction of the statue, said: "It was broken from its Pedestal and broken in Pieces, and we hear the Lead wherewith this Monument was made is to be run into Bullets." The *New Hampshire Gazette* of July 20, 1776, published a letter from New York dated July 11, reading: "Last Monday evening the equestrian statue of George III, which tory pride and folly raised in the year 1770, the SONS OF FREEDOM laid prostrate in the dust, the just desert of an ungrateful tyrant. The lead wherewith the Monument is made is to be run into Bullets, to assimilate with the brains of our infatuated adversaries, who, to gain a pepper-corn, have lost an empire."

While it is not recorded who were the actual leaders in the achievement of this act of disenthrallment, and it seems impossible to verify, from any of the records of the time, the family tradition that Hercules Mulligan was the one who proposed it and was one of those who led the movement, it would be quite characteristic of an Irishman to propose or take part in so daring an enterprise. From the newspapers of the day we also learn, that during the reading of the Declaration a violent thunder storm came up, which dispersed the people to their homes, but in the evening they again assembled in "The Common," where the sole topic of conversation was the immortal document and an exchange of opinions among the patriots as to what action the British army would take. The people paraded "The Broad-Way 5"; a great crowd collected in "The Common"; bonfires were lighted and torches flashed; the windows were illuminated; the taverns were crowded with excited patrons, and we are told "the shouts of the multitude responded to the deep tones of the rolling thunder." The people could not restrain their enthusiasm, and no doubt it was in the midst of this excitement that attention was called to the statue of the King, which the patriots had looked upon since its erection six years before as a defiant symbol of English power, with the result that the proposition to tear it down was taken up in earnest by the excited citizens. Nine days after this event, the people were requested through a notice in the Packet , [3] to assemble at the City Hall, "where the Declaration of the Independency of the United States will be published," and the same paper of July 25, 1776, gave the following account of this meeting:

"Thursday last the DECLARATION of the INDEPENDENCY of the UNITED STATES OF AMERICA was published at the CITY HALL, where a number of people, true friends of the rights and liberties of this country, attended and signified their approbation to it by loud acclamations. After which the Coats of Arms of his Majesty George the III, were torn to pieces and burnt in the presence of the spectators."

On August 22, 1776, or about one week before the battle of Long Island, an English fleet under Admiral Howe landed a formidable force of trained regulars on the outskirts of Brooklyn," and it became a matter of much quiet discussion among American officers as to whether the army should retain the position it then occupied on Long Island and give battle to the enemy, or retire to the higher and more favorable ground on Manhattan Island. Alexander Hamilton at this time having been only a Captain of Artillery, was not high in the councils of the military chiefs, but he was fully acquainted with the precarious position of the American forces and evidently had very practical ideas as to the course that should be taken. And on this point the "Narrative of Hercules Mulligan" sheds some interesting light.

According to the "Narrative," Alexander Hamilton, John Mason, Philip Rhinelander, Colonel John Lamb and others held a conference at Mulligan's house, "previously to the skirmish on Long Island." On this occasion Mason and Hamilton, "lamenting the situation of the army on Long Island," determined to write "an anonymous letter to General Washington pointing out their ideas of the best means to draw off the army." Hamilton was the writer of the letter, which Mulligan states was read in his presence, and "after it was finished" he intrusted Mulligan with the delicate mission of conveying it "to one of the family of the General," which he relates he did in good season. If Mulligan's recollection of this incident, and his "impression that the mode of drawing off the army which was adopted was nearly the same as that pointed out in the letter," were correct, it is seen that he was the bearer of a most important communication on this occasion.

[1] *Minutes,* etc., London, 1786. Copy at New York Historical Society.
[2] *New York Gazette and Weekly Mercury,* August 28, 1775.

[3] Samuel Loudon, the editor and publisher of this paper, was a native of Belfast, Ireland, and was a patriot of the Revolution. Its first number appeared on January 4, 1776, but in September of that year, when the British took possession of the city, Loudon was compelled to remove his printing-press to Fishkill on Hudson where he continued the *Packet* until November, 1783, when he returned to the City and resumed its publication. Loudon was an ardent Irishman and gave much space in his paper to despatches from Ireland concerning "Grattan's Volunteers" and the proceedings of the Irish Parliament. He also published many articles encouraging the movement for Irish independence.

[4] In his biography of General Sir William Howe (New York, 1932), Bellamy Partridge shows that there were "400 transports, ten ships of the line, twenty frigates and some 1200 big guns under the command of his brother, Admiral Lord Richard Howe, and his own (General Howe's) forces of about 28,000 well-trained and equipped men."

Chapter Seven

WHEN the Americans were defeated at the battle of Long Island their situation became extremely hazardous, for the English fleet was still in the bay and in position at any moment to sever all communication between New York and Brooklyn. During a night of fearful anxiety to Washington and his staff (August 28, 1776), a Council of War was held, at which the "anonymous letter to General Washington" was considered, and as a result of their deliberations it was unanimously decided to draw off the troops and retreat across the East River to the fortifications at McGowan's Pass and the upper end of Manhattan Island. On the night of the 30th, the movement was carried out successfully, to the great mortification of General Howe and the probable salvation of the American army. [1]

Lieutenant-Colonel James Chambers of the First Regiment of the Pennsylvania Line, in a letter [2] dated "Kingsbridge, September 3, 1776," said:

"It was thought advisable to retreat off Long Island, and on the night of the 30th it was done, with great secrecy. Very few of the officers knew it until they were on the boats, supposing that an attack was intended. A discovery of our intention by the enemy would have been fatal to us. The Pennsylvania troops were done great honor by being chosen the corps de reserve to cover the retreat. The regiments of Colonels Hand, Magaw, Shee and Haslet were detailed for that purpose. We kept up fires with outposts stationed until all the rest were over. We left the lines after it was fair day and then came off. Never was a greater feat of generalship shown than in this retreat, to bring off an army of twelve thousand men, within sight of a strong enemy, possessed of as strong a fleet as ever floated on our seas, without any loss, and saving all the baggage. General Washington saw the last over himself."

The retreat from Long Island was one of many bold strokes executed by Washington during the war, and which proved him a master of strategy. And it is worthy of mention that all four commanders of the troops assigned to the important work of covering the retreat were countrymen of Hercules Mulligan. [3] Colonel Hand was a native of Clyduff in Kings, now Offaly, County, Magaw of Strabane, County Tyrone, Shee of Westmeath and Haslet of the City of Dublin, Ireland.

George Washington Parke Custis, grandson of Mrs. Martha Washington, has given us an interesting account of the incident of the letter from Hamilton, above referred to, and he also verifies the statements of the authorities already quoted as to Washington's honoring Hercules Mulligan so signally after the evacuation of New York by the British, on November 25th, 1783. In his *Recollections and Private Memoirs of Washington*, Custis states:

"Hamilton's talents were apparent in very early life. Previous to the battle of Long Island he crossed over to Brooklyn, and thence, by examining the positions of the American forces with a military eye, he became convinced that with such materials as composed the American army, a conflict with troops which consisted of all soldiers would be hopeless of success. Filled with these ideas, Hamilton addressed an anonymous letter to the Commander in Chief, detailing many and forcible arguments against risking an action, and warmly recommending a retreat to the strong grounds of the main land. The letter created no little surprise in the mind of the General, but it was mixed with respect for the talent displayed by the writer. The disastrous battle of Long Island is a matter of history.

"The letter of which we have made such honourable mention was forwarded to the General by M---, afterwards celebrated for having conveyed to the American Commander the most important information during the occupancy of New York by the British army. The morning after Washington made his triumphal entry into the City of New York, 25th, November, 1783, he breakfasted with M---, to the wonder of the Tories and the perfect horror of the Whigs." [4]

In view of the statement in the "Narrative of Hercules Mulligan," there can be no question as to who Custis meant by "M---," although why he referred to Mulligan by the initial only is not clear. There can be little doubt also as to the source of his information, *i.e.*, that it was obtained from Washington himself. Custis' father was Colonel John Parke Custis of the Revolutionary army, son of Mrs. Washington by her first husband, and after the war, while Washington was President of the United States, Custis lived in the "President's Palace" [5] as one of the family. Washington appointed him an executor of his will and left him a handsome estate at Arlington, on which he lived until his death in 1857. It is strange that in an enlarged edition of Custis' *Recollections*, published in New York in 1860, the entire paragraph relating to Hercules Mulligan having been the bearer of the letter from Hamilton to Washington, of his "having conveyed to the American Commander the most important information" concerning the enemy, and of Washington breakfasting with him on Evacuation Day, was eliminated! The 1859 edition, in which the above-quoted statement appears, was the first publication in book form of Custis' *Recollections*. The *Recollections* appeared originally as a series of articles by Custis in the *National Intelligencer* of Washington, D. C.

When Washington retreated from Long Island, he crossed the East River from the foot of the present Fulton Street to Whitehall Street. He endeavored, without success, to rally his forces in a cornfield at what is now the neighborhood of 42nd Street and Fifth Avenue, and at this point he is said to have had a narrow escape from capture. The historians agree that were it not for the clever stratagem of the famous Mrs. Murray, in entertaining the English officers in her house near the river, Washington and his staff inevitably would have become prisoners of the British on this occasion. The main body of the British army landed at Kip's Bay, or about the foot of the present 34th Street, on September 15th, 1776. At that time many of the citizens, whose sentiments toward the revolutionary cause were well known, were marked men, and I venture to say that Hercules Mulligan was among the number, for he had made himself particularly obnoxious to the Tories during the early activities of the Sons of Liberty. Seeing that the capture of the City was inevitable, an exodus of the patriots set out from New York, and it was on this occasion that Mulligan, with his wife and boy, the latter only two years old, was apprehended. A fortunate circumstance for Washington, as events proved.

There are no records which would indicate the exact date, or under what circumstances, Hercules Mulligan became the confidential correspondent of the Commander-in-Chief, and except in two instances it seems impossible to determine what means he adopted to convey his communications through the enemy's lines. However, it is noted that in Mulligan's "Narrative," he says: "after the British crossed the Hudson at Fort Lee I went to see my young friend (Hamilton) and found him encamped near General Washington, having the command of his company," and that he "afterwards saw him when he came to New York with a flag (of truce) to see Sir Guy Carlton." It was on November 18, 1776, two days after the surrender of Fort Washington, that the British under Cornwallis crossed the Hudson to Fort Lee, which Washington had abandoned. The records show that Hamilton's artillery company was then at Hackensack, five miles from Fort Lee, with the main body of the American army, and when Washington a few days later was informed of the approach of Cornwallis to the American camp, he ordered a retreat to the Delaware River. While it is not possible to determine the date and place of Mulligan's visit to Hamilton, it was probably about November 20, 1776, at the camp in Hackensack.

Mulligan had been released from prison only one month before, and being still under surveillance, naturally he had to be extremely wary in his movements. The "Narrative" does not state how he managed to leave the City and reach the American lines on the occasion of his visit to Hamilton. That detail he probably deemed unnecessary to mention, since the "Narrative" was written for the benefit of the Hamilton family, and an endorsement on the document shows that it was intended mainly as an account of his relations with Alexander Hamilton in his young days. The condition of the document indicates that it was written at different times. The incidents which it relates are not arranged in chronological order, and, as will be seen from the accompanying reproduction, portions of it are now very obscure on account of the fading of the ink.

Nor is the exact purpose of his visit to Hamilton, or what conversation he had with him when he "afterwards saw him when he came to New York," disclosed in the "Narrative," and Hamilton's biographers make no mention of these incidents. It is clear that it was with Hamilton the idea originated, of the possibility of securing information as to the movements of the enemy, and it is very probable that on one of these two occasions he broached the subject to Mulligan, and that the latter, in turn, discussed it with his brother, Hugh. Chief Justice Shea and John C. Hamilton agree that it was "after Hamilton entered into the family of Washington" that Mulligan became "the confidential correspondent of the Commander-in-Chief." Hamilton received his appointment to Washington's staff on March 1st, 1777, and it is probable that about that time Washington discussed with Hamilton the advisability of employing some trusted agent who would keep him informed of the situation in New York. One of the family says that Mulligan was recommended by Hamilton for this work, not only because of the confidence he reposed in his friend and compatriot, whom he knew would enjoy this post of danger, but because he also knew that Hercules' brother was in constant touch with the British officials and army officers, and through this means he had unusual opportunities for securing useful information. But whatever way it came about, there can be no doubt that it was the fidelity and zeal with which Mulligan executed his task, that prompted Washington at the first opportunity to publicly acknowledge his patriotic services.

Lossing informs us that when the British felt themselves firmly seated on Manhattan Island after the fall of Fort Washington, they leisurely prepared for permanent occupation, by strengthening the intrenchments across the island and erecting barracks, and speedily placed the army in comfortable quarters. Nearly all the Whig families whose means permitted them had left the City, and their deserted homes were taken possession of by the officers of the army and the refugee loyalists. Churches were devoted to military purposes, and spacious prisons were erected for the American captives when the cells of the City Hall and the provost prison were full. Every pleasure that could be procured was freely indulged in by the army; all sorts of amusements were prepared, and for seven years the City remained a prey to the licentiousness of strong and idle detachments of a well-provided army. New York was the headquarters of British power in America during that time, and here the most important schemes for operations against the patriots, military and otherwise, were planned and put in motion. The municipal government was overthrown, martial law prevailed, and the business of the City degenerated almost into the narrow operation of suttling. Here many petty depredating expeditions were planned, and from New York many a vessel departed with armed troops to distress the inhabitants of neighboring provinces, or with secret emissaries to discover the weakness of patriot camps, to encourage disaffection in the Republican ranks, and by the circulation of spurious paper money and lying proclamations, to disgust the people and win their allegiance to the Crown. [6]

How important it was to Washington, that every available item of information regarding the enemy's movements in New York should be transmitted to him with the least possible delay, can best be understood when we consider these facts. And the fact that he placed such great confidence in Mulligan, and through him in his brother, Hugh, is a circumstance well worthy of mention in any history of the American Revolution. Yet, both have been ignored, not only by our City historians but in every history of the Revolution!

It is known that during the Revolutionary struggle, there were instances of men whose services at critical moments, in obtaining information for the Commander-in-Chief, had been of the greatest importance, and indicating that frequently such services were undertaken at great personal risk and from the most disinterested love of country. The men engaged in this character of work were selected chiefly for their shrewdness and fearlessness, their contempt of danger and, perhaps, their love for adventure. Necessarily, they had to be men whose mental faculties were of a high order and equal to emergencies. Their lives were constantly in peril, for such information, to be of any value from a military standpoint, could only be secured by the exercise of the most subtle and skilful artifice, in which the slightest error might mean discovery and instant death. For the soldier fighting in the ranks there is honor and glory, and perhaps reward; if he perform some heroic deed, he receives the commendation of his superiors and the applause of the public; if he fall, it is within sight of his comrades in arms and his name will be enrolled among his country's patriots. But, for the secret military agent, there is no glory; his work must be done in silence and perhaps without hope of ultimate reward or the plaudits of his countrymen! And when, in such a case as that of Hercules Mulligan, the agent is one who has a substantial business built up by years of industry, yet is willing to take chances to lose it all if he can only serve his country's cause, his sacrifice is all the more and such truly heroic conduct merits a comparatively greater measure of praise.

[1] *Memoirs of the Long Island Historical Society;* Vol. 3, p. 222.
[2] See *Pennsylvania Archives;* 5th Ser., Vol. 2, pp. 610-612.
[3] It should be mentioned also, for the information of those who believe that the Irish had no part in the War of the Revolution, that the troops under the command of Colonels Hand, Magaw, Shee and Haslet were comprised largely of Irishmen or sons of Irish immigrants. This statement can be verified by reference to the rolls of these regiments in the State Archives at Harrisburg, Pa.
[4] *Recollections and Private Memoirs of Washington;* p.51 Washington, D.C. 1859.
[5] The name originally applied to the Executive Mansion, or "White House."
[6] Lossing, *Field Book of the Revolution;* Vol. 2, pp. 835-6.

Chapter Eight

MEAGRE though our information is as to the activities of Hercules Mulligan, as the secret agent of the beloved commander of the patriot forces, there is ample opportunity, if one were so disposed, for drawing upon the imagination as to the extent and character of the services he rendered. As much, for instance, as there was for Cooper in his immortal romance of *The Spy*, for it is known that Cooper's sole foundation for his creation of the character of "Harvey Birch" was the mere statement made to him by Governor Jay that there was such an individual in Washington's employ. Beyond this fact, we are assured that Governor Jay furnished Cooper with no details, and all other incidents in the tale were the novelist's personal inventions. [1]

"George Washington's Accounts with the United States," during the eight years of the war, are among his papers at the Library of Congress. In these accounts there are entries of several large payments on account of "secret services," but the names of the recipients are not given in any case, for extreme care necessarily had to be exercised to surround the names with secrecy. These accounts show that Washington "expended for secret intelligence" a total of £2102 10s., and there is a "note" in his handwriting, reading thus:

"Before these accounts are finally closed, justice and propriety call upon me to signify that there are Persons within the British Lines, if they are not dead or removed, who have a claim upon the Public under the strongest assurances of compensation from me for their services in conveying to me private Intelligence, and which when exhibited I shall think myself in honor bound to pay. Why these claims have not made their appearance ere this, unless from either of the causes above mentioned , or from a disinclination in them to come forth till the B. force is entirely removed from the United States, I know not. But I have thought it an encumbent duty on me to bring the matter to view, that it may be held in remembrance in case such claims should hereafter appear.
G. W "

This note was written in the year 1783, at which time New York was still the headquarters of the English army; so, therefore, there can be little doubt that among the "Persons within the British Lines" who had furnished intelligence, one of those whom Washington had in mind was Hercules Mulligan. Colonel Benjamin Tallmadge, who had charge of the "Intelligence Department" after 1777, says in his *Memoirs* that the Revolutionary agents within the British lines used fictitious names and a disguised handwriting in all of their correspondence. Custis says in his *Recollections* that "the business of the secret service was so well managed, that even a suspicion never arose as to the medium through which intelligence of vast importance was continually being received in the American camp from the very Headquarters of the British army."

According to a story related many years after the war by John W. Mulligan, son of Hercules, it was known to the family that his father was in touch with a Revolutionary agent in Long Island. He frequently absented himself from home, and on one occasion he had a narrow escape from a Tory patrol in the vicinity of Hempstead. This agent was Abraham Woodhull, known to history as "Samuel Culper." Among the Tallmadge papers, there is a letter from "Culper" dated October 31, 1778, to the effect that he was cooperating with "a faithful friend and one of the first characters in the City," who was "making it his business to keep his eyes open upon every movement and assist me in all respects, and meet and consult weekly in or near the City." The inference is that they were laying plans how best to obtain information, and in view of the statement of John W. Mulligan, there can be very little doubt that the person whom "Culper" referred to was Hercules Mulligan.

It is possible that a prolonged and minute search through the 212 volumes that cover the Revolutionary War part of the Washington papers, might reveal some clue as to Mulligan's activities, but I have been unable to undertake so great a task. The intelligence system of the Revolution appears to have been somewhat loosely managed until Tallmadge was put in charge, and even he did not control all lines of communication leading to Headquarters. The cavalry outposts on the lines everywhere usually were channels of secret information, and some of the commanding officers of Departments had means of their own of obtaining information and their own private correspondents. Washington strictly forbade all mention of personalities in reports to him and insisted, either that there should be no signatures to such reports, or that they be signed in fictitious names already agreed upon, on account of the danger to his friends and informants. [2] It is easy to understand, therefore, why no official record was retained of Mulligan's services and why any written reports which he may have furnished to the Commander-in-Chief are not now obtainable. Doubtless, it was the rule for military commanders to destroy such documents and keep the information strictly to themselves; at least that would be an obvious precaution.

Prior to the Revolution, the British commissariat had large dealings with the house of Kortright and Company, and during the seven years that the British army had possession of the City, Hugh Mulligan, who was then the sole owner of the business, was on friendly terms with General Clinton's subordinates, and it was chiefly through this connection that his brother, Hercules, succeeded in ingratiating himself with the army officers. Besides, some of the army officers were billeted in the Mulligan home, [3] and as many of them were patrons of "the fashionable clothier," as Hercules was called, we can readily see that he was in a peculiarly advantageous position to accomplish his purpose, and we can depend upon it that he took every opportunity to improve the acquaintance. While we can never know how he managed to secure information from this source, we may be permitted to visualize scenes of the "matching of the wits" between the enthusiastic and resourceful Irish patriot and the English officers who patronized his establishment, and how he wormed out of the unsuspecting Englishmen information relative to intended movements of the enemy that was of great military value to Washington and his staff.

The "Liberty Boys" derived considerable merriment and satisfaction in devising schemes to discomfit the Tories. In 1778, Lord Rawdon, a Tory leader, tried to raise a regiment in New York, to be called "The Volunteers of Ireland." Extraordinary efforts were made to secure recruits; various tricks and cajoleries were resorted to; generous bounties and large pay were offered freely. In a letter to Lord George Germain, Secretary of State for War, in October, 1778, General Clinton expressed the hope that he would obtain the required quota to fill up the regiment "from the emigrants from Ireland," who, he explained, "kept up their national customs," and "to work upon this latent seed of national attachment" appeared to him "the only means of inciting these refugees to a measure contrary perhaps to the particular interests of most of them." According to Rivington's paper, the *Royal Gazette,* on March 17, 1779, the officers of the garrison collected as many Irishmen as they could muster, and "accompanied them to the Bowery," where "dinner was provided, consisting of five hundred covers," and "the Anniversary of St. Patrick, Tutelar Saint of Ireland, was celebrated with accustomed hilarity."

Clinton appointed a Major John Lynch chief recruiting officer, with instructions "to work among the Irish." Meanwhile, the "Liberty Boys" were not inactive; they secretly distributed leaflets advising resistance to the recruiting officers, and although the part actually played by Mulligan is not known, the situation gave him an opportunity to exercise his persuasive talents among his countrymen. On one occasion, he had an altercation with Lynch in a tavern in King Street, and on the following day he was summoned to military headquarters and interrogated about his "obstructing Major Lynch in the performance of his duty." But, with his usual faculty for getting out of tight places, nothing came of the enquiry. General Clinton's efforts to recruit the regiment proved a failure, and in 1781, when "The Volunteers of Ireland" were in South Carolina, as part of the forces of Lord Cornwallis, they mustered only 83 men. [4]

During the war several attempts were made by British and Tories to capture prominent American leaders, and in referring to an attempt in the month of January, 1779, to seize Governor Livingston of New Jersey, John C. Hamilton relates an incident that reflects considerable credit on the alertness and loyalty of Hercules Mulligan. Hamilton states: "A similar design was formed on the person of Washington. He had appointed to meet some officers at a designated place. Information was given by a female in the tory interest and the necessary arrangements were made to seize him, but timely intelligence frustrated the attempt. A partisan officer, a native of New York, called at the shop of Mulligan late in the evening to obtain a watch-coat. The late hour awakened curiosity, and after some enquiries, the officer vauntingly boasted that before another day they would have this rebel General in their hands. This staunch patriot, as soon as the officer left him, hastened unobserved to the wharf and despatched a billet by a

negro, giving information of the design." [5] John C. Hamilton does not refer to any particular authority for this interesting statement, but when we bear in mind that he knew Hercules Mulligan well and that the family papers show that John W. Mulligan was an intimate friend of both Alexander Hamilton and his son, it is evident the latter had a means of obtaining the information from first hand sources. Mulligan's negro servant, whose name has been handed down in tradition as "Cato," was under suspicion for a long time, and when his absence from New York on several occasions was noted by General Clinton's spies, he was put under constant surveillance. At one time, when returning to Mulligan's home, he was arrested when stepping out of a boat in the East River, and questioned as to the business on which his master sent him out of town, but the faithful negro refused to divulge, and he was thrown into prison and treated with great cruelty.

In February, 1781, another attempt was set on foot by the enemy to seize General Washington, but owing to the vigilance of the Mulligan brothers this scheme was providentially discovered. At this time Washington was about to make a journey into New England which would take him along the Connecticut shore, and the fact becoming known to General Clinton he despatched a body of cavalry by way of Long Island Sound for the purpose of intercepting him. Hugh Mulligan received a hurried order to place a quantity of provisions on board the boats which were to carry the horsemen up the East River, and thus learned of the importance of the enterprise, and no sooner had the detachment left New York than he informed his brother Hercules, who quickly conveyed the news to American Headquarters, then in the vicinity of West Point. The result was that Washington and his staff took a roundabout way of reaching their destination, and thus frustrated the designs of the English General. This incident was mentioned in a letter from Washington to Lafayette, dated New Windsor, February 25, 1781, and in a footnote in the *Writings of Washington* [6] it is thus referred to: "...Intelligence had come from New York that 300 horsemen had crossed over to Long Island and proceeded eastward and that boats had at the same time been sent up the Sound. It was inferred that this party would pass from Long Island to Connecticut and attempt to intercept General Washington on his way to Newport, as it was supposed his intended journey was known to the enemy. Lafayette suggested that the Duke de Lauzan should be informed of this movement as soon as possible that he might be prepared with his cavalry, then stationed at Lebanon, to repel the invaders."

Several instances can be quoted to indicate the unceasing watchfulness of Washington's secret agent in New York. Dr. Smucker shows in his *Life of Alexander Hamilton*, that while the British had possession of the City both

Hamilton and Washington "corresponded regularly with some intimate friend and confidant in this City," whom, however, he fails to mention by name. Among the "Official Papers of Major-General Alexander Hamilton" at the Congressional Library, there is a letter from him to a Committee of Congress, dated Morristown, N. J., April 5, 1777, in which he referred to some information that had reached him from New York, that the British intended "to embark 3000 men on board transports, then lying off Staten Island," which his informant "conjectured was with a view to the Delaware." There is also a letter from Hamilton to General Gates, dated Peekskill, November 12, 1777, referring to some "facts well ascertained" to the effect that "New York had been stripped as bare as possible and that in consequence of this the few troops there and the inhabitants are under so strong apprehensions of an attack as almost to amount to a panic, and that to supply the deficiency in men, effort is making to excite the citizens to arms for the defence of the City."

Justice Thomas Jones also relates an incident, proving that some person in New York was constantly furnishing intelligence to General Washington, of a character that could only be secured from some "inside" source. Jones was Recorder of the City and Justice of the Supreme Court of the Province of New York, and between 1783 and 1788 he wrote a history of the City, in which he related many details that came under his personal observation. In referring to the work of the secret agents employed by Washington, Jones quotes a statement made by Stephen Moylan, [7] Colonel of the Fourth Dragoon Regiment of the Continental Army, which statement, he says, was related to him "by a gentleman who was a prisoner in Connecticut during the winter of 1779," and was to the effect that "not a return of the number and state of the British army at New York had been made to General Clinton for the last two years, but that General Washington received a copy in 24, or at most in 48, hours after its delivery to the Commander-in-Chief." [8] In 1779, Moylan's regiment was stationed at Fairfield, Conn., about forty miles from New York, at which place he was frequently in contact with friends in the City. In a report from Moylan to General Washington dated Greenwich, Conn., August 13, 1779, relating to secret intelligence he had secured from enemy headquarters, he said that certain information he had sent to him at Amboy the previous year, "came from persons employed within the City." We have no means, however, of knowing if Mulligan was one of those with whom he was in contact.

Information as to the enemy's movements in the field was also communicated from New York at various times. For example, on October 21, 1777, a large body of troops which had just arrived to reinforce the British army, embarked at New York and "passed up the East River in a multitude of flat-bottomed boats and other vessels," and although this movement must, necessarily, have been carried out with great secrecy, the news was known to General Washington before the flotilla had passed out of Long Island Sound.

Dr. Smucker does not inform us who the "intimate friend and confidant in this City" who "corresponded regularly" with Hamilton and Washington was, and Justice Jones failed to mention the name of the person who supplied the important news spoken of by Colonel Moylan's informant. Yet, in the light of our information as to the position occupied by Hercules Mulligan at this time, of his known earnestness and activity as a patriot and his eagerness to serve his country's cause, these statements are of peculiar significance, for information of such character could come only from the City of New York and from one who made it his business to secure it for some special purpose. And what is more likely than that it originated with the man who, we are told, was "the confidential correspondent of the Commander-in-Chief" in this City?

In this connection, some of Washington's letters excite most interesting reflections. In a letter dated July 14, 1778, to Count D'Estaing of the French fleet, Washington informed him of "advice just received (from New York) that the enemy are in daily expectation of a provision fleet from Cork, and that they are under great apprehensions lest it should fall into your hands." [9] From White Plains on August 28th of the same year, Washington wrote General Heath "...By several late accounts from New York there is reason to believe that the enemy are on the point of some important movement. They have been some days past embarking cannon and other matters. Yesterday, 140 transports fell down to the Hook. These and other circumstances indicate something of moment being in contemplation," etc. [10]

[1] The authority for this assertion is Miss Susan Fenimore-Cooper, daughter of the great novelist, in an article contributed by her to the *Atlantic Monthly* for February, 1881.

[2] Tallmadge once incautiously mentioned the name of one of his agents, and in the Washington Papers the name is so heavily scored over by the pen of the Commander-in-Chief as to defy deciphering, and Washington's letter to Tallmadge contains a sharp rebuke for having needlessly exposed the spy to such a risk of discovery.

[3] In Rivington's *Royal Gazette* of March 8, 1780, and other issues, it is stated that the officers of the 17th Regiment of Foot were quartered in Mulligan's home at 23 Queen Street.

[4] When the "regiment" left New York for Charleston in July, 1780, it numbered "253 rank and file." (Beatson's *Naval and Military Memoirs;* Vol. vi, app. 211; London, England, 1790-1804.) Rawdon took them to the Irish settlement at Waxhaw, N. C., "thinking," wrote he to Cornwallis, "as it was an Irish corps, it would be received with a better temper by the settlers of that district, who were universally Irish and universally disaffected." But, he had "the fullest proof that the people who daily visited my camp not only had constant correspondence with the rebel militia, but used every artifice to debauch the minds of my soldiers and persuade them to desert from their colours." (See copy of Rawdon's letter to Cornwallis, in *Hartley's Life of General Francis Marion,* p. 130.) So many deserted from the "Corps," that Rawdon announced: "I will give the inhabitants ten guineas for the head of any deserter from the Volunteers of Ireland and five guineas

only if they bring him in alive"! Toward the end of 1780, the "Corps" numbered 127 men, and in the next year, when it was reduced to the strength of one company, Lord Rawdon threw up his commission in disgust and sailed for England. (See *A Hidden Phase of American History,* by Michael J. O'Brien, pp. 186-194, for a more complete account of "The Volunteers of Ireland.")

[5] *History of the Republic of the United States of America, as traced in the Writings of Alexander Hamilton;* Vol. 1, p. 527, Philadelphia, 1864.
[6] Collected and edited by Worthington C. Ford; Vol. IX, p. 166; New York, 1890.
[7] Colonel Moylan, at one time, was Aide-de-Camp to General Washington. See numerous letters from and to him while acting in that capacity, in Force's *American Archives;* 4th Ser., Vols. IV and V. He was a native of the City of Cork, Ireland, and was a brother of the Catholic Bishop of that Diocese.
[8] Jones, *History of New York During the Revolution;* Vol. 11, p. 210.
[9] *Writings of General Washington;* Vol. VII, p. 101.
[10] *Ibid.,* pp. 166-7.

Chapter Nine

ONE of the most timely and important pieces of information which Mulligan is known to have secured was in July, 1780, when he learned that General Sir Henry Clinton was planning an attack on the French troops in Rhode Island with 10,000 men. Mulligan conveyed this information quickly to General Washington, then in camp at the Highlands of the Hudson, the result of which was that Clinton's expedition utterly failed. Among the Washington Papers there is a letter from him to Lafayette on July 22, 1780, wherein he said: "Colonel Hamilton informed you yesterday of the advices received from New York of an intended embarkation said to be destined for Rhode Island." That Washington received further information from New York of the actual sailing of the expedition, is shown by his letter to Rochambeau on July 31, 1780, to the effect that "Sir Henry has sailed with the principal part of his force to attack you, 8000. Am glad the inactivity of the enemy has given you time to prepare." Menaced on sea and land, General Heath, the American commander at Rhode Island, secured reinforcements of Massachusetts and Connecticut Militia and prepared for Clinton. When Clinton arrived in Huntington Bay in Long Island Sound, he was apprized of the situation in Rhode Island, and as a consequence he abandoned the expedition and returned to New York.

A passage in Washington's letter to the President of Congress from "Headquarters, Passaic Falls, 15 October, 1780," is also significant. This letter reads in part: "I enclose your Excellency a New York paper of the nth., which contains nothing material except Arnold's address to the inhabitants of America. [1] I am at a loss which to admire most, the confidence of Arnold in publishing it, or the folly of the Enemy in supposing that a production signed by so infamous a Character will have any weight with the people of these States, or any influence upon our Affairs abroad. Our accounts from New York respecting the intended embarkation continue vague and contradictory. A few days ago it was said that the troops designed for the expedition [2] were all on board and that the Fleet would sail immediately. I last night received intelligence that the troops were again disembarked and that a plan entirely new was in agitation. Unluckily, the person in whom I have the greatest confidence is afraid to take any measure for communicating with me just at this time, as he is apprehensive that Arnold may possibly have some knowledge of the connexion and may have him watched. But, as he is assured that Arnold has not the most distant hint of him, I expect soon to hear from him as usual." [3]

Who was the person in New York in whom Washington had "the greatest confidence," and why was he "afraid to take any measure for communicating with him at this time"? Winthrop Sargent, in his Life of Major John Andre, [4] clearly intimates that it was Hercules Mulligan, and the reason for this temporary cessation of his despatches to Washington is explained, not only by the traditions of the Mulligan family, but by John C. Hamilton in his *History of the Republic of the United States of America.* [5]

When Arnold's treason was discovered (September 25, 1780), he took refuge on board a British warship lying in the Hudson River near West Point, which brought him immediately to New York, where he was appointed a Brigadier-General of the British army. [6] Having enjoyed the confidence of Washington and other officers of high command, there can be no doubt that Arnold had knowledge of Mulligan's work, for one of his first acts on establishing himself in the City was to have Mulligan placed under the strictest surveillance. When the news of the execution of Major Andre (October 2, 1780), reached New York, we are told "the loyalists raised a great outcry for revenge," and the British troops demanded that they be led to the attack of Washington's camp, then only twenty-five or thirty miles up the Hudson River, and, as related by Sargent in his *Life of Andre,* [7] "the Commander-in-Chief could hardly keep the soldiers within the bounds of discipline."

There were certain persons in New York whose sympathies toward the American cause were well known and some of whom were suspected of "aiding the enemy." An account of the execution of Andre, in Holt's *New York Journal and General Advertiser* of October 9, 1780, then published at Fishkill, said: "We further learn that the truly infamous Arnold, through whom this unfortunate gentleman lost his life, has lodged information against sundry persons in New York, supposed friendly to our cause, in consequence of which upwards of fifty of them were imprisoned." House to house visits were made by the City Marshal and his aids, and much ill-feeling was created against the authorities, even on the part of loyalist families, and among the fifty or more persons arrested and imprisoned was Hercules Mulligan. His brother had received an inkling from an army officer of the intended raids, but although Hercules fully expected to be taken into custody he decided to remain, on the chance that if Arnold's expedition soon left New York he might be able to ascertain its intended destination, and convey this information to Washington. That was not to be, however; Mulligan was arrested by Major-General Jones in person, and, as we shall see, his apprehension was considered of especial importance.

He was brought under guard to the City Bridewell, which stood on the north side of Murray and Great George's Streets, or Broadway. It was a two-story building, the second floor being divided into wards, one of which was set apart for "desperate criminals," and it was here that Mulligan was confined. One of his descendants relates that "on the third day of his confinement he eluded his jailer and dropped into the yard. But luck was against him, and when, in the very act of climbing over the wall into an adjoining garden, the guard was just being changed and the luckless prisoner was returned to his cell." Thence he was transferred to the notorious Provost Prison, then located where the Hall of Records now stands, at the corner of Centre and Chambers Streets. He was arraigned before a court-martial and the principal witness to appear against him was Benedict Arnold. But, although Arnold pressed the charge vigorously and presented to the officers of the court-martial what he insisted was presumptive evidence of the prisoner's guilt, he was unable to convict the prisoner, and that fact, in itself, is an indication of the cleverness of Mulligan in hoodwinking the military authorities and covering up the evidence of his "guilt." How long he remained a prisoner is not disclosed by any available records, but the fact that he lost his business about this time, as indicated in the family papers, would make it appear that he must have been detained for a considerable time, and that he passed through a period of great danger.

In referring to the secret agents employed by Washington, Winthrop Sargent says: "One whose observations, perhaps on occasion, saved Washington's life, was able by his connections with the West Indian house of Kortright and Company, to unsuspectedly pick up much useful information for our army. Yet his character was so little affected by these transactions, that he remained the valued friend of both Hamilton and Washington, and it was perhaps, to set his patriotism straight in the public view that our General on the final entrance into the City took his first breakfast at his house. Arnold had him seized and tried hard to hang him, when he came over, but there was not enough evidence." [8]

This statement clearly identifies "the valued friend of both Hamilton and Washington" as none other than Hercules Mulligan, whose "connections with the West Indian house of Kortright and Company," through his brother, Hugh, already have been established. And in this statement, and in that of John C. Hamilton relative to Mulligan's imprisonment at the very time that Washington wrote the President of Congress about the dearth of intelligence from New York, we have the explanation of Mulligan's temporary inactivity in communicating intelligence to the Commander-in-Chief. We can well believe that Arnold would hang him if he could, because nothing better illustrates the innate meanness of the traitor than his informing the British after his treason of the names of the men who befriended him in Canada in 1775-6. The evidence of this infamy, only a little less in degree than his treason to his country, is contained in the papers of General Haldimand. In the *Pennsylvania Magazine of History,* [9] there is an article on "General Haldimand in Pennsylvania," in which the damnable charge frequently made against Arnold is sustained.

Winthrop Sargent's account of the honor done to Mulligan on Evacuation Day would make it appear that, during the war he had masqueraded before his fellow citizens as a loyalist; that consequently Washington thought it necessary to rehabilitate his friend in the public eye, and that it was with that end in view he publicly repaired to the Mulligan home on Evacuation Day and breakfasted with the family. All of the information that I have been able to ascertain, however, seems to disprove that assumption. (1) Mulligan was well known to a large number of the citizens as one of the "Liberty Boys"; (2) it was known that he was a friend of Alexander Hamilton and other leading patriots and that Hamilton had lived in his house; (3) the Tories probably were aware through the public agitation preceding the war that he took part in the work of the Revolutionary Committees; (4) the exciting incidents of the election on March 6, 1775, at which Mulligan was present, were known to the loyalists; (5) in all likelihood the part he played in the destruction of the statue of King George was known; (6) he was a member of the committee appointed by the Provincial Congress, which tried the Tories for treason in 1776 and had sternly reproved Forbes, the leading Tory; (7) he and his friend, Victor Bicker, organized a military company in New York four months after the outbreak of the Revolution; (8) the part played by him in the removal of the cannon from the Battery on November 23, 1775, undoubtedly was known to the citizens; (9) in July, 1776, he co-operated with Alexander Hamilton in recruiting his company of artillery; (10) when he left the City with the American troops later in the same year, he was seized by the Tories and brought back; (11) he was arrested again four years later at the instance of Benedict Arnold and placed on trial for "treason"; (12) there is a tradition in the family that he was known to the British officers as "rebel Mulligan," and lastly, it is questionable that an Irishman of his temperament and sentiments, who had thrown himself into the forefront of the agitation which preceded the Revolution, could have been able to drown his patriotic fervor to such an extent as to create the impression among his fellow-citizens that he had all along been a loyal subject of King George.

Therefore, there cannot be the slightest doubt as to Washington's motive in associating himself with the Mulligan family on Evacuation Day. It was simply to make public acknowledgment of his thanks to his faithful Irish friend for the services he had rendered, work which he well knew could not have been performed except at the risk of his life. There is a family tradition that General Washington was accompanied by some of the officers of his staff; and that his visit to the Mulligans created jealousies among some of New York's prominent citizens, is apparent from George Washington Parke Custis' comment, before quoted, about "the horror of the Whigs."

The military authorities pretended to cease watching Mulligan after his release in 1780, but as a matter of fact they never relaxed in their suspicions of him, and an incident is related by one of his descendants which indicates that he was under surveillance until the close of the war. To some it may be a surprise to learn that about this period many Irishmen in America were members of the Masonic fraternity; there was then no interdiction against Catholics joining that Order. For example, the first lodge of Masons in the Province of New York was at Johnstown in 1767 and was called "St. Patrick's Lodge," and there were several Irishmen on its roll, Catholics and Protestants. Sir William Johnson, a Protestant from County Meath, Ireland, was its presiding officer and Michael Byrne, a Catholic and a native of Wicklow, was its "Junior Warden." At Portsmouth, N. H., in 1780, there was also a "St. Patrick's Lodge" and in New York City there was an "Erin Lodge." Mulligan was a member of a New York lodge, which used to meet in John Street between Broadway and Nassau Street. Although he was known to the military officers as "rebel Mulligan," it is obvious they had no actual knowledge of the role he was playing as confidential agent of General Washington, notwithstanding that in 1780 Benedict Arnold had him arrested and put on trial for "treason." Near the close of the war, suspicion was again strongly directed toward Mulligan, and on one occasion, it is related, "a Tory in the pay of the enemy chased him down Great George's Street and into John Street. Mulligan took refuge in the building where the Masons met and burst into the room as the lodge was in session, with the Tory after him in hot pursuit. The Tory was also a member of the Order, so there was nothing for it but to desist, and thus the redoubtable Mulligan escaped from what probably would have been serious consequences!" Only a short time after this exciting incident, Mulligan was signally honored by no less distinguished a Mason than Washington himself, when, on Evacuation Day, November 25, 1783, after the victorious American troops were reviewed on the Bowling Green, he took breakfast with the Mulligan family at their home, No. 23 Queen Street, now 218 Pearl Street.

[1] A copy of Arnold's "Address to the Inhabitants of America," dated October 7, 1780, may be found in Rivington's *Royal Gazette* of October ii, 1780. It contains more than a thousand words. The *Royal Gazette* of October 25, 1780, and every issue of that paper for two months, also published Arnold's "Proclamation to the Officers and Soldiers of the Continental Army, who have the real Interest of their Country at Heart and who are determined to be no longer the tools of Congress or of France." It is amusing to note from this document that one of the grave charges Arnold brought against the American Congress was in these words: "Do you know that the eye which guides this pen lately saw your mean and profligate

Congress at Mass for the soul of a Roman Catholic in Purgatory, and participating in the rites of a Church against whose anti-Christian corruptions your pious ancestors would have witnessed with their blood!"

[2] An expedition intended for Virginia, under the command of the traitor, Arnold, then a Brigadier-General in the English service.
[3] *Writings of Washington;* Vol. VII, pp. 496-8.
[4] P. 441.
[5] Vol. 1, p. 46.
[6] *Life and Treason of Benedict Arnold,* by Jared Sparks; p. 249; New York, 1856.
[7] p. 403.
[8] *Life of Major John Andre,* by Winthrop Sargent; p. 441.
[9] Vol. 29, pp. 307-9.

Chapter Ten

As already stated, about three years before the close of the war Mulligan lost his business as a result of his imprisonment by the traitor, Arnold, and the continued hounding of him by the military authorities. His fortunes seem to have varied with the vicissitudes of the times, and after his release he was employed for a time by his brother, Hugh, which is the probable explanation of the statements already quoted as to his having been "connected with the house of Kortright and Company." In 1783, advertisements in the newspapers show that he was engaged in the real estate business at number 23 Queen Street, but two years later his name appeared in a list of "insolvent debtors" published in the *Packet.* In 1786, according to the City Directory, he was again in business as a "merchant taylor."

The references to him in the newspapers and in the public records after the Revolution, are sufficient to show that he was a public-spirited citizen and that he took more than a passive interest in current affairs of the City and State. In the Manuscript Department of the State Library at Albany there is on file a document (No. 2403), entitled "Petition to the Council for the Temporary Government of the State, 1783." It bears the signatures of ninety-three citizens of New York styling themselves "the Whig members of the Episcopal Church," who, according to *Rivington's Gazette* of October 10, 1783, held a meeting "at Simmons' Tavern in New York," at which James Duane presided. Some of the signers of this document were:

Hercules Mulligan	Hugh Hughes	John Keating
Edward Fleming	"Patt" Dennis	
James Duane	Peter Hughes	

Another interesting document in the State Library (No. 2405) is a "Petition for Confirmation of Certain Wardens and Vestrymen of Trinity Parish," which was "read and committed to a Committee of the whole House" on February

24, 1784, and duly approved by the Legislature. Among the twenty Vestrymen nominated in the Petition appears the name of Hercules Mulligan, and there is an entry in the parish books recording his appointment as Vestryman on April 17, 1784. Among the signers to this Petition were:

John Conway	Peter Hughes	William Mooney
"Patt" Dennis	William Leary	Edward Phelan
John Fleming	Patrick McDavitt	

There is also at the State Library a "Petition of the Old Vestry and their Friends for the Endowment of a Separate Church," dated February 28, 1784, which was read in the Senate on March 5th of that year. It is comprised of six separate documents, numbered 2406 to 2411 inclusive, and among the citizens of New York who signed it we find

Robert Carr	Benjamin McDowell	Michael Moore
John Fleming	Hugh McDowell	Thomas Moore
Anthony Ford	Robert McGinnis	Richard Mulheran
John Healy	William McGinnis	Hercules Mulligan
Philip Kearney	John McKenahan	Thomas C. Murphy
Thomas Lowrey	John McKenny	Michael T. Reiley
Thomas Lynch	Daniel McNeil	Thomas Roach
William McCarter	Edward Mooney	Miles Sherbrooke
John McClenahan	William Mooney	Oliver Templeton
Robert McCormick	James Moore	Thomas Welsh

In accordance with this request, the Legislature on April 17, 1784, passed "An Act for making such Alterations in the Charter of the Corporation of Trinity Church as to render it more conformable to the Constitution of the State." Paragraph No. 4 of the Act reads in part as follows:

"Be it therefore further enacted, and it is hereby enacted by the authority aforesaid, that James Duane and Robert R. Livingston be the present Church-Wardens of the said Corporation, and that Anthony Griffiths, Hercules Mulligan, Marinus Willet, John Stevens, Robert Troup, Thomas Tucker, Joshua Sands, Richard Morris, Francis Lewis, Lewis Morris, Isaac Sears, Daniel Dunscomb, William Bedlow, William Duer, John Rutherford, Anthony Lispenard, Thomas Grennell, William Mercier, Thomas Tillotson and Christopher Miller be the Vestrymen of said Corporation."

Dr. William Berrian [1] says that Hercules Mulligan served as Vestryman until 1788; Dr. Morgan Dix, in his church history, [2] says he served "from 1784 to 1787" but a "List of Vestrymen in Succession at Trinity Church," which I have examined at the office of the Corporation, indicates that Mulligan was elected for the term "1784 to 1786" only, and there is no entry in the vestry books showing that he served for a second term. Onderdonk, the New York historian, also mentions Hercules Mulligan as one of "the well-known and honored citizens of New York who were Vestrymen of Trinity Church in 1784." [3]

As Vestryman of Trinity, he took part in the promotion and education of a church choir. The lack of appropriate instrumental and vocal music had been the subject of discussion by the Vestry, and in 1785 we find Hercules Mulligan bringing the matter to a head by the introduction of a resolution, at a meeting of the Vestry, "to establish a school of church music where the younger members of the congregation could be trained by a professional instructor." A committee of citizens of various denominations was formed, who undertook to raise a fund for the support of the school, and the *New York Packet* of January 8, 1786, published an address, "To the Lovers of Church Music," signed by fifteen prominent citizens, one of whom was Hercules Mulligan. This resulted in the organization of competent choirs, not only in Trinity but in several other New York churches. In 1799, Hercules Mulligan is mentioned as a member of "The Uranian Society for the improvement of Church Music," [4] and in view of the report in the

Name	Year admitted	Name	Year admitted
William Adair	1770	Michael Flynn	1794
Bartholomew Barnwell	1788	John Gillis	1773
George Barnwell	1780	Nathaniel Haley	1792
Richard Blake	1772	Walter Haley	1786
John Brandon	1777	John Hanifen	1800
Thomas Buckley	1801	John Healy	1770
John Butler	1782	Archibald M. Kearney	1806
Thomas Butler	1782	Samuel Kelly	1782
William Butler	1772	Patrick Kennan	1791
John Byrne	1773	James Kennedy	1806
Peter Cargill	1774	Thomas Kennedy	1770
Thomas Carberry	1788	William Kennedy	1774
John Casey	1782	Jeremiah King	1792
Fleming Colgan	1770	Francis Lynch	1793
John Connor	1773	William McAdam	1772
James Croker	1782	George McAvoy	1773
Thomas Cunningham	1773	Andrew McCormick	1780
Patrick Dennis	1770	William McCormick	1800
James Devereaux	1771	Hugh McCreedy	1774
Joseph Dillon	1772	Bernard McDavitt	1773
Simon Donnell	1780	Charles McDonald	1775
Thomas Doran	1770	Robert McEaver	1787
John Duffey	1794	James McEvers	1791
Thomas Duggan	1782	James McEwen	1780
Robert Dunlevy	1801	Neil McHenry	1786
Henry Ennis	1781	Edward McKellar	1775
Edmond Fanning	1796	Thomas McKenny	1781
Henry Fanning	1797	John McNeil	1780
Nathaniel Fanning	1791	George McSweeney	1791
Richard Fanning	1794	Nicholas Moran	1802
Joshua Farrell	1800	John Mulholland	1789
William Fitzpatrick	1798	James Murphy	1797
Peter Murphy	1798	John Reardon	1780
Anthony Neill	1789	Isaac Riley	1795
James Neill	1794	Patrick Roach	1798
Terence O'Brien	1799	Thomas Roach	1771
John O'Bryan	1792	Myles Sherbrooke	1770
Thomas O'Bryan	1794	Dennis Sinnot	1787
John O'Connor	1795	John Welch	1771

ON THE HONORARY MEMBERSHIP ROLL

Name	Year admitted	Name	Year admitted
Michael Boyle	1791	John McAdams	1778
John Cockran	—	Alexander McComb	1788
Michael Connor	1772	Daniel McCormick	1770
James Constable	1791	Patrick McDavitt	1771
William Constable	1791	Charles McEvers	1770
William Cunningham	1777	John McKenny	1773
John Davan	1773	Dennis McReady	1773
James Duane	1785	John McVickar	—
Hugh Gaine	1771	Cooke Mulligan	1772
John Gilliland	1773	Hercules Mulligan	1772
John Keefe	—	Daniel Neil	1772
Henry Kelly	1772	Carlisle Pollock	—
John Kelly	1780	David Reedy	1791
Samuel Loudon	1791	Cornelius Ryan	1776
Dominick Lynch	1788	Oliver Templeton	—
Thomas Lynch	1772	Hugh Wallace	1770

Packet above referred to, it is probable that he was a member before that time.

In 1772 Hercules Mulligan was made an honorary member of "The Marine Society of the City of New York," organized in 1769 "for the relief of distressed shipmasters or their widows and children," and "for the promotion of maritime knowledge." Here again we find him in distinguished company, since some of the foremost citizens of New York were members of the society, and in 1783 General Washington and George Clinton were elected to honorary membership. In that year Captain Thomas Roach, an Irishman, was elected to the presidency of the society, and in 1792 Thomas Roach was president of the Society of the Friendly Sons of St. Patrick. Three of the charter members of the Marine Society were Thomas Doran, Patrick Dennis and Myles Sherbrooke, all natives of Ireland, and announcements in the newspapers show that for many years the society met "at the house of Captain Thomas Doran in Water Street," and after his death "at the Widow Doran's." The roster of this society is an object lesson to those who entertain the idea that no Irish came to New York before the nineteenth century. Its regular membership was comprised of masters of vessels plying out of New York and merchants engaged in commerce in this City, and in its oldest existing list of members we find a number of Irish merchants and sea-captains.

In 1776, Mulligan was a member of an association, called "The New York Society for Employing the industrious Poor and promoting Manufactory," organized by a number of merchants. An unconfirmed tradition in the family also says that he was a member of the Society of the Friendly Sons of St. Patrick, organized in New York on March 17, 1784, but it is not possible to verify this from the records of the society, because of their destruction in a great fire which occurred in New York in the year 1835. But it is entirely probable that the tradition is correct, since there are indications that Daniel McCormick, the founder and first president of the society, had close business relations with Hugh Mulligan, and several of those known to have been on its earliest membership roll were among Hercules' personal friends and associates.

In 1786, Hercules Mulligan was a member of the "Society for Promoting the Manumission of Slaves in the City of New York," founded by Alexander Hamilton, and of which John Jay was president, and John Keefe, [5] a leading lawyer, and who in 1790 became a "Justice for Trial for Civil Causes," was secretary. [6] At one of the meetings of the society, held at the Merchants' Coffee House, it was resolved to send a Memorial on the subject to the Senate and Assembly of the State of New York, and in the *Packet* of March 13, 1786, there is a copy of this Memorial and the names of its signers. In referring to the treatment of slaves, the subscribers said that "although free by the laws of God, they are held in slavery by the laws of the State"; they pointed out "with pain and regret the miseries which those unhappy people experience from the practice of exporting them like cattle and other articles of commerce to the West Indies and the Southern States," and they pleaded strongly with the Legislature "to prohibit a commerce so repugnant to humanity and so inconsistent with the liberality and justice which should distinguish a free and enlightened people." A large number of citizens joined in this Memorial, and among its signatories, besides Hercules Mulligan, are noted such names

Alexander Hamilton	Richard Varick	John Cortlandt
John Jay	Henry Rutgers	William Depeyster
James Duane	Robert Benson	Samuel Ogden
Nicholas Fish	Nicholas Romaine	Marinus Willet
John Lamb	Henry Remsen	James Beekman
William Constable	Cornelius Roosevelt	Samuel Loudon

and many others, all of them conspicuous figures in New York history. Seven members of the Livingston family also signed this Memorial, and that Hercules Mulligan's friends were men of that stamp, we may judge from an account of a controversy in the year 1785 between Brockholst Livingston [7] and one Abraham Smith.

During the trial of a suit in the County Court, Smith's father, a New York lawyer, was accused of "interfering in a non-professional manner" with Brockhoist Livingston. A bitter altercation took place between Livingston and Smith at the Merchants' Coffee House, which created a considerable furore, and the former announced through the Daily Advertiser that "this has led to the necessity of reminding the public of a trait in this young man's character, which, but for his impertinent behaviour, might in time have been buried in oblivion." It appears that Smith had pretended to sympathize with the patriot cause, and in the year 1779 he approached Baron Steuben and represented himself as a sufferer at the hands of the British, and that he wished to attach himself as a volunteer to the General's staff. Steuben accepted his professions of patriotism, although Smith's real purpose was to obtain information for the enemy, and when his object was accomplished he deserted the patriot army and joined the corps commanded by the traitor, Arnold. These facts were generally unknown to the public and Livingston determined "to* make a complete exposure of Smith's conduct," and with that end in view he called on "his friends, Morgan Lewis, [8] Baron Steuben [9] and Hercules Mulligan, to testify to their knowledge of Smith's actions during the Revolutionary War." The *Daily Advertiser* of October 4, 1785, published a long statement of the case from Livingston, appended to which were statements signed by Lewis, Steuben and Mulligan, certifying to the character of Smith. Mulligan's testimony was as to his "'having seen Smith in the City dressed in the uniform worn by Arnold's Corps" and that "Smith made no secret of his being an officer with said Corps."

In official papers relating to the historic controversy during the Revolutionary period between New York and the District of Vermont, over land grants and boundaries, which appear in the "Records of the Governor and

Council of the State of Vermont," Hercules Mulligan is also mentioned. With John Jay, Alexander Hamilton, Marinus Willett, Robert Troup, Hugh Gaine, Henry Remsen, Nicholas Cruger, Frederick Rhinelander, John Kelly [10] and others he was interested in lands on the east side of Lake Champlain, granted to them by the Province of New York, but the title to which was disputed by Vermont. On February 23, 1789, Mulligan joined with the other grantees in a Memorial to the Legislature praying for the appointment of "Commissioners with full power to treat of and agree to the independence of that District" (Vermont), which resulted in the passage of an Act in October, 1790, under which Vermont was to pay these claimants a sum of $30,000. to reimburse them for their rights and interests in said lands. [11]

In 1798, Hercules Mulligan was a member of a benevolent and provident organization called "The General Society of Tradesmen and Mechanics," incorporated under an Act of the Legislature in March, 1792. Among his fellow members, we find

James Byrne	Francis Lynch	Peter McEachern
John Connor	Joseph Lyons	John McGowan
Peter Conrey	Walter McBride	William McKenny
John Cummings	Peter McCartey	Nicholas Meade
John Cunningham	John McComb	William Mooney
Richard Cunningham	George McCoy	William Mooney (2)
James Duffy	James McCullen	James Moore
John Fitzpatrick	Andrew McCready	John Moore
Benjamin Gallaher	Dennis McCready	William Rutledge
John Gilmore	James McCready	Thomas Ryan Benjamin
James Hayes	Robert McDowel	Sullivan Michael White

[1] *Historical Sketch of Trinity Church;* New York, 1847.
[2] *History of the Parish of Trinity Church;* New York, 1898.
[3] *New York City in Olden Times,* by Henry Onderdonk; p. 71.
[4] *The Commercial Advertiser* in 1799 shows that Peter Conrey, a New York Alderman, was president of the Uranian Society at this time.
[5] See New York City Directory for the year 1786. Also Greenleaf's *New York Journal and Weekly Register* of May 24, 1787.
[6] In a long article in the *Freeman's Journal* of Philadelphia, on May 16, 1787, Hercules Mulligan, John Keefe and William Keefe were listed as members of the society; and in a report in the same paper on May 30, 1787, John Duffy was so listed.
[7] Brockholst Livingston was a son of Governor William Livingston of New Jersey and grandson of Philip, Second Lord of the Manor of Livingston in Columbia County. He was a Colonel of the Revolutionary army, was made a Judge of the New York Supreme Court in 1802 and in 1806 he became an Associate Justice of the Supreme Court of the United States.
[8] Morgan Lewis was a prominent lawyer at this time. In 1792 he became Chief Justice of the New York Supreme Court and in 1804 Governor of the State.

[9] Baron Steuben was Commander of Artillery in the Army of the Revolution.
[10] John Kelly was a New York lawyer, "an Irishman of ability and standing" (Hall's History of Eastern Vermont).

[11] *Records of the Governor and Council of the State of Vermont;* Vol. III, p. 448; Montpelier, Vt., 1875. See also Hall's *History of Eastern Vermont;* Vol. II, p. 604.

Chapter Eleven

As is to be expected of an Irishman, Mulligan was active in New York politics of the post-Revolutionary period, having been one of the charter members of the "Society of Tammany or Columbian Order," and for many years he and his son, John W. Mulligan, were in opposite camps in the field of politics. At first, the Tammany Society drew largely from the Sons of Liberty, which organization, after the establishment of peace, having accomplished its object, went out of existence. Most of the charter members of the Society had been on the Revolutionary Committee of Correspondence, of which Hercules Mulligan was a member in 1775, and, in fact, the organization of the Sons of Liberty was sometimes called "The Sons of Saint Tammany." The constitution of the Tammany Society shows that Hercules Mulligan was among the signatories, and the family papers also indicate that he was an intimate friend of William Mooney whom history credits as the founder of the organization. Mooney was an ardent member of the Sons of Liberty, and a New York historian refers to him as "a violent Liberty Boy." [1] He was the first Grand Sachem of the Tammany Society, which was formed at a meeting held in the City Hall, then at Wall and Broad Streets, on May 12, 1789, or about two weeks after Washington had taken the oath of office as the first President of the United States. Benjamin Strong, whose sister, Charlotte, married Hercules Mulligan's son, William C., was secretary of the society in 1792. In February, 1808, Mulligan was one of the committee appointed by the Tammany Society, to make arrangements respecting the interment of the relics of the American soldiers and seamen who perished on board the prison ship, *Jersey,* in New York harbor, and at the laying of the cornerstone of the monument (April 13, 1808), he marched in the great procession of the citizens through the streets of New York.

It is noted that in none of the accounts herein quoted the place where Washington breakfasted with the Mulligan family on November 25, 1783, is mentioned. However, there is not the slightest doubt that their home at that time was at number 23 Queen Street, and Joseph A. Scoville, one of the accepted authorities on New York history, in his Old Merchants of New York, [2] says that "Mulligan lived during the war at 23 Queen Street, only a few doors from Pine," then known as "King," and that "he was one of the most fashionable merchant tailors in his day." Rivington's *Gazette* of November 15, 1783, carried the following advertisement: "To be Sold. A House, number 20

New Street, next to the corner of Wall Street; an indisputable title will be given. Enquire of Hercules Mulligan, number 23 Queen Street." *The New York Packet and Daily Advertiser* of November 20, 1783, also published this advertisement: "I intend to sail for England in a few days; therefore request all those indebted to make immediate payment to Mr. Hercules Mulligan, No. 23 Queen Street, or to Mrs. Mary Quain, 57 Cherry Street, they being authorized to receive the same. And all those who have any demands will please to call immediately for payment at number 57 Cherry Street. Thomas Quain."

Since it is thus shown that Mulligan's home was at 23 Queen Street on November 20, 1783, it is safe to say that he lived there on Evacuation Day, five days later. At that time the present Pearl Street was known as "Pearl" from State to Broad only; from Broad to Wall it was called "Dock Street," and from Wall to Chatham, where it ended, it was called "Queen." After the war, the City Fathers eliminated from the nomenclature of our streets all names savoring of royalty. Thus, all such names as "Queen," "King" and "Crown" were discontinued and the three streets first mentioned— which were really, as they are now, one continuous thoroughfare—were amalgamated into the present name of Pearl Street. [3] Queen Street began at Wall, and according to the real estate records, the northerly corners of Wall and Queen seem to have followed the same line then that they do now; so that, accepting Scoville's statement that Mulligan's home was "only a few doors from Pine," we are able to identify 23 Queen Street as on the present Pearl Street block, a short distance north of Pine Street.

The records of the Tax Department and of the Surrogate's office afford a means of identifying the location of Hercules Mulligan's home. The oldest existing tax record is the assessment roll of the year 1789. It is arranged by Wards, and in the descriptions of the properties assessed the street numbers are given, and that portion of Queen Street between numbers 1 and 30 is shown as in the East Ward. According to the "certificate of Daniel McCormick, [4] Assessor for the East Ward," the house known as number 23 Queen Street was then owned by Francis Moyoning and on the 1791 tax book the property was again assessed to Moyoning, with Francis Bassett recorded as the occupant of the premises. The records of conveyances show no transfer of the property from Moyoning, but at the Surrogate's Office [5] there is a copy of the will of "Frances Moyon," dated July 2, 1792, under which she bequeathed to her "kind and affectionate friend, Francis Bassett of the City of New York, Pewterer," her house and lot "in which he and I now live," and which is described in the will as "on the south easterly side of Queen Street."

While there are no lot numbers shown on the tax books of this period, the records indicate that the house numbers on Queen Street ran consecutively, beginning with the first house on the northeast corner of Wall, and running to the northerly end of the street, thence down the west side, not as at the present time with the odd numbers on one side and the even numbers on the opposite side. So that, in those days we had what now seems a curious situation as to street numbers, namely that number 20 Queen, for example, was directly opposite 238 on the same street. This I have verified in other ways. The "Fly Market," one of the old landmarks of the district, which was on Queen Street just north of Maiden Lane, was much used in advertisements of business houses in the neighborhood to bring to the attention j of the public the location of the advertisers' premises. For instance, there was an advertisement in the *New York Gazette* and *Weekly Mercury* in 1778 which said that 22 Queen Street, on the east side, was "near the Fly Market," while an advertisement in the *Royal Gazette* in the year 1780 said that number 208 Queen, on the west side, was "opposite the Fly Market."

On referring these facts to the Title Guarantee and Trust Company, for verification, they inform me that old No. 23 Queen Street is the present No. 218 Pearl Street. It may, therefore, be accepted as an established fact that the present 218 Pearl Street is the spot where the home of Hercules Mulligan stood and where the immortal Washington breakfasted with his faithful Irish friend, on the morning of that eventful day in American history when this country cast off the British yoke for all time.

This part of the City was originally one of the fashionable residential quarters and it remained so for some years after the Revolution. Queen was then a very different street from what it is today. The thoroughfare that is now covered by the noisy Elevated railroad and which is mostly given up to businesses carried on in old buildings sadly in need of repair, was then lined with shade trees and on part of its route were the residences of some of New York's leading citizens. Mrs. Martha J. Lamb, the New York historian, tells about "the fine homes in Dock Street, the southern part of Queen, quite pretentious in appearance, with deep balconies overlooking the bay," and that "the lower part of Queen Street was dotted with elegant-looking mansions and shaded with fine trees. This street was built up much earlier than Broadway and some of its houses stood nearly three quarters of a century." The old Depeyster mansion on Queen Street she points out as an example, with "its grounds covering a block or more, with coach house and stable in the rear, and in the same street, not far away, was the town house of Andrew Elliot, Collector of the Port, and the City home of the Brevoorts, with its lilies and roses in the front yard." The house which occupied the present number 168 Pearl Street, on the block below 23 Queen, in 1789, is described by Mrs. Lamb as "an elegant old mansion," and "it was here that Governor George Clinton lived at the time of the inauguration of our first President and where Washington, as President-elect, and the Committee by whom he was received dined on the 23rd of April, 1789, the day of his arrival in New York from Mount Vernon." [6] Shortly after that date, Washington took up his residence nearby, at the Walter Franklin house on the corner of Cherry and Pearl Streets.

The Mulligans were neighbors of some famous New Yorkers. At 27 Queen Street in 1783 was the home of William Bayard; three years later Abraham

Brevoort was at 26 Queen, and the famous Isaac Sears was at 30 Queen. Edward and William Laight were on Queen Street near Maiden Lane and in the immediate neighborhood were the residences of Lewis Ogden, Peter McDougall, Nicholas Hoffman, James Barclay, the Ludlows and Bleeckers, and Peter Goelet kept "at the sign of the Golden Key" nearby at 48 Hanover Square, Aaron Burr once lived at number 10 Cedar Street, and in William, the nearest parallel street to Queen, some time later, were the homes of Lafayette and Washington Irving. In 1786, Jacob Astor advertised his musical instrument store at 81 Queen Street, while Richard Varick, a distinguished lawyer and at one time Mayor of the City, lived at number 11 Queen, and further down on Dock Street, the continuation of Queen Street, were the handsome residences of Hugh and Alexander Wallace, both natives of Ireland. They were merchants of wealth and position, and we are told "the mansion of Hugh Wallace was the resort of the great dignitaries of the Province and his manner of life was costly and elegant." [7] The home of the famous Walton family in 1772 was on the corner of Wall and Queen Streets, "the magnificence of which is said to have led to the enactment of the Stamp Act." [8]

However, there seems to have been little to admire in the plan of some of the City's streets and highways in those days, and some announcements in the newspapers indicate that fashionable private residences, merchants' stores, lawyers' offices and mechanics' workshops ranged along in unseemly juxtaposition. The principal streets were Pearl and Queen, as well as Great Georges' Street, or "The Broad Way" as it was sometimes called, and from which our main artery since took its name. "The Broad Way" had well-shaded sidewalks and there were several fine residences of notable New York families along the lower part of the street that is now lined with "skyscrapers." From the rear of the houses on the west side of Broadway, as far up as St. Paul's Chapel, gardens were laid out on the slope which ended on a sandy beach, and the street commanded a delightful prospect of the town and the Hudson River. On the cross streets, from the present City Hall Park to the Battery, the merchants lived over their shops, though on John, Fulton, Beekman, Gold and Cliff Streets east of Broadway, there were also many private residences. What a remarkable transformation to the present condition of these streets!

In the *Packet* of November 21, 1788, and in five succeeding issues of the paper there was an advertisement by Mulligan's attorney requesting "all persons having any demands against Hercules Mulligan, either by bond, note or book debt, to deliver their respective accounts properly attested to Edward Dunscomb [9] at number 45 Maiden Lane." The same paper of May 1, 1789, contained an announcement by "Hercules Mulligan, one of the petitioning creditors of Dennis Lott," giving notice "to all creditors of Dennis Lott of Flat Bush in Kings County, Yeoman, an insolvent debtor, that they shew cause before the Honble John Sloss Hobart, Esqr., at his Chambers in Crown Street, before the 15th, of May next, why an assignment of said insolvent's estate should not be made and the said insolvent discharged." These advertisements would seem to indicate that Mulligan was about to retire from business at that time.

However, the City Directory for 1789 and 1790 gives his home address at 30 Golden Hill (John Street), later as 160 Broadway, and in 1792 and for some time after 1800 he lived at the corner of Vesey Street and Broadway, where the old Astor House was afterwards erected. At the latter address he also had some distinguished neighbors, for only one door from the corner of Vesey Street, at 221 Broadway, was the official residence of Aaron Burr when vice-president of the United States, and at 223 Broadway was the home of Edward Livingston, then Mayor of the City. He was one of the guests invited by Mayor Livingston to the ceremonies incident to the laying of the cornerstone of the City Hall on May 2 6, 1803. A copy of an illustration is here reproduced from Valentine's *Manual,* showing Saint Paul's Chapel and the neighborhood of Vesey Street and Broadway. The Museum building opposite, that is, on the corner of Ann Street and Broadway, was known in Revolutionary times as "Hampden Hall," and it was here that the "Sons of Liberty" had their headquarters after 1771. It was the scene of action of many of the riots and public disputes which characterized that era in the history of the City. Perhaps nothing can give us a better idea of what the appearance and extent of the little City was at this time, than the fact that there was then a signboard at the corner of Vesey Street and Broadway bearing the inscription, "Road to Albany," and at the opposite side, where the St. Paul building now stands, there was a sign pointing out to the traveler the "Road to Boston!"

Hercules Mulligan was not listed in the City Directory between 1803 and 1817, but during the next three years he reappears with his address as 173 Fulton Street. The last year in which his name appears in the Directory was 1820 at 27 Murray Street and his residence at 280 Bowery Road, so I assume it was in that year he retired permanently from business, having been then eighty years old. The Bowery at that time was nothing like the busy thoroughfare that it became in later years, for while there were plenty of shops along its route, there was a sort of suburban picturesqueness to the street, with its fine old trees, shaded residences and gardens stretching back to the river. Now its vicinage is a region of narrow streets and thousands of tenements, where are gathered representatives of every race in Christendom and where there are as many languages and dialects spoken as in Continental Europe! Truly, "Time is the great architect of change!"

The closing years of his life were spent quietly at the home of his son, John W. Mulligan, which was then at number 20 Cedar Street. Eighty-five years were the measure of his days, and on the 4th of March, 1825, surrounded by his sons and grandchildren, the old patriot surrendered his spirit into the hands of his Maker. To the last he was full of reminiscences of Alexander Hamilton, and as John C. Hamilton writes, "he lived long enough to speak to other generations of his friend, the great man that was untimely taken away."

In the New York newspapers of the time there are no obituary notices of his death, beyond a mere announcement of which the following, taken from the *New York Advertiser* of March 9th, 1825, is a copy: "Died on Friday morning, in the 85th. year of his age, Mr. Hercules Mulligan." As already stated, his last years were spent in the solitude of his home and, doubtless, having passed out of the memory of the younger generation, he belonged to "the forgotten past," and no particular notice was taken of his demise by the newspapers. This will be understood readily when we consider the fact that when he first settled in New York its population was only 9000, and in the year of his death it was 166,000. [10]

[1] Goodwin's *Historic New York;* Vol. 2, p. 52. Mooney's advertisements in the New York newspapers show that he was an importer of rugs, carpets, furniture and household goods, with a shop at 23 Nassau Street.

[2] Scoville wrote under the pseudonym, "Walter Barrett." He was City Clerk for many years and his work exhibits a most intimate knowledge of events during the first quarter of the nineteenth century, and that he was personally acquainted with the leading families and business men of the City. He was also a personal friend of Hercules Mulligan's sons, John W. and William C. Mulligan. His great work was published in four volumes in New York between 1864 and 1866.

[3] Queen and King were changed to Pearl and Pine Streets respectively in 1794. In the New York *Minerva* of December 19, 1794, a tory citizen made a violent protest against the change and although he took his protest before the Common Council it was of no avail.

[4] In tracing the footsteps of Hercules Mulligan, a striking fact that presents itself to the author is the frequency with which Irish-named residents of the City are met with in the records and old newspapers. The records of deeds and conveyances at the Register's Office for the City and County of New York contain upwards of 750 legal instruments executed prior to the year 1800, mostly covering transactions in real estate, in which people of Irish names were the principals, either as grantors or grantees. And among the members of the Chamber of Commerce in the year 1779 were seven New York merchants who were natives of Ireland (see *Colonial Records of the New York Chamber of Commerce,* 1768-1784, by John Austin Stevens; N. Y., 1867). No New York historian has considered these facts of sufficient importance to give them even passing mention, and thus they have led readers of history to believe that all of the early inhabitants of this City were people of English and Dutch descent. The Daniel McCormick above mentioned was a native of Ireland and for many years was a leading New York merchant. He was the first President of the Society of the Friendly Sons of Saint Patrick on its foundation in New York in the year 1784.

[5] Liber 42, p. 331.

[6] *Magazine of American History;* Vol. XXI, No. 3.

[7] Mrs. Martha J. Lamb, *History of the City of New York.*

[8] *Historical Guide to New York City,* by Frank Bergen Kelley, published by the City History Club.

[9] Edward Dunscomb was a lawyer and was Hercules Mulligan's brother-in-law.

[10] *Valentine's Manual* for 1845.

Chapter Twelve

HUGH MULLIGAN, father of Hercules, originally was of the Catholic faith, but like almost all Catholics in America at that period, having no means of practicing their religion, in course of time they associated themselves with other churches. Hercules Mulligan became an Episcopalian and he and his son, John W. Mulligan, attended Trinity Church, but the family of his second son, William C., were Presbyterians. The New York colonial records contain several thousand of the most distinctive Irish names of persons who were undoubtedly of the Catholic faith. New York Catholics had no chance to practice their religion, however, until November, 1783, after the British evacuated New York, [1] and in these liberal times it is curious to read how John Leary, a resident of Leary Street [2] between 1760 and 1772, "used to make the trip to Philadelphia once a year to attend the holy sacrifice of the Mass!" Until the close of the Revolutionary War and while the English laws were in force, no Catholic clergymen were allowed to officiate in this Province or State, [3] and Watson in referring to religions in New York in colonial times, says "a man did not dare avow himself a Catholic; it was odious and a chapel then would have been pulled down." [4] The Catholic Church in New York was not incorporated until June ioth, 1785, and its first pastor was Revd. Charles Whelan, an Irish Capuchin, who had served as a Chaplain in Admiral De Grasse's fleet during the War of the Revolution, and who was recommended to New York Catholics by General Lafayette. [5] [6]

It is an interesting fact also, notwithstanding the general idea that prevails among historians that the organization of the Sons of Liberty excluded Catholics from membership, that William Mooney, the Revolutionary patriot and one of the staunchest "Liberty Boys" in New York, was a regular communicant at Saint Peter's Catholic Church after 1785 and in 1789 his name is listed among the Vestrymen of that Church . [7] But, although it is probable Hercules Mulligan was baptized in Ireland in his father's faith, he did not follow the example of his friend, Mooney, possibly for the reason that he had been for so many years associated with Trinity Church.

The Sanders family, into which Hercules Mulligan married, had a vault in Trinity churchyard, and his sister-in-law, Mrs. Ann Sanders Livingston, was baptized in the first church. The original edifice was destroyed in the great fire of 1776, and, according to a document in the handwriting of William Mulligan, son of Hercules, now in the possession of Mrs. Fanning, his great-granddaughter, the Sanders vault originally was at the rear of the church on the Trinity Place or west side. Although there is a Mulligan family vault in Trinity churchyard, Hercules' remains were buried in the Sanders vault. Many years ago, when the edifice was enlarged, several graves and vaults were covered over by the new addition and among these was the Sanders vault. Thus it happens that the Sanders vault is directly under the chancel of the present church, and the circumstance that the remains of the American Irish patriot rest in this spot is regarded as a considerable distinction.

At the office of Trinity Church Corporation there is a "Record of Burials," with copies of the inscriptions on the tombstones. It contains records of the burials in Trinity and Saint John's churchyards of ten of the Mulligan family, among them the wife and several children of Hercules, and the entry relating to his wife reads: "1826, September 27, Elizabeth Mulligan, aged 79 years." In the "Record of Vaults" at Trinity there is no copy of the inscription on the Sanders' vault, but on a diagram of the church building this vault is shown to be under the chancel, which confirms the information furnished by Hercules Mulligan's descendants as to the present location of the vault. I am informed at the Comptroller's office of Trinity Church Corporation that when this record was begun the alterations in the edifice had already been made and the vaults covered over, which explains why a copy of the inscription on the vault containing Hercules Mulligan's remains is not now available. An entry in the burial register of Trinity Parish indicates that Hercules Mulligan was buried "in St. John's," at Hudson and Varick Streets. But that entry evidently was an error, since the record as to his remains having been placed in the Sanders vault in Trinity churchyard was made by his son, William.

The Mulligan family vault is on the Rector Street side of the churchyard. Alongside it is the grave of Hugh Gaine, the Belfast newspaperman who founded the *New York Mercury* in 1752, and only ten paces behind it is the grave of Hercules' friend, Alexander Hamilton, and the monument erected to the memory of that distinguished statesman by the corporation of Trinity Church. Game's grave is at the edge of the pathway on the Rector Street side, and directly opposite it on the other side of the path, is the tomb of Robert Fulton of steamboat fame, whose father was a native of Kilkenny, Ireland. The Mulligan vault is covered by a slab, which, although now considerably discolored by the ravages of time, seems to have been originally of white marble and on it is this simple inscription, without date:

"WHALIE [8]
and
MULLIGAN'S
VAULT"

In this famous church, less than one hundred feet from one of the busiest thoroughfares in the world, on the same level with some of the distinguished scions of the nobility of Europe, and surrounded by the graves of men and women who were famous in the early history of the American Metropolis, lie the remains of the American Irish patriot, Hercules Mulligan. Nor is Hercules Mulligan wanting for Irish neighbors, for in Trinity churchyard are several slabs and headstones bearing old Irish names. Many of the memorials of the dead scattered through this old cemetery are not now decipherable, for they have succumbed to the effects of time and are gradually crumbling away, but from such of the inscriptions as are readable, may be noted many familiar Irish names. [9] In some instances, the place of nativity of the deceased is given as "Ireland," and the periods of interment run from as early as 1708 to the year 1820.

In the "'Manual of the Corporation of the City of New York," [10] by David C. Valentine, there is a copy of a poster which was distributed among the citizens on November 24, 1783, announcing the formation and route of the procession held on the first Evacuation Day, which indicates that the cavalcade, after proceeding through the Bowery, passed down Queen Street to the Battery. A writer on "Old New York" refers to the morning of November 25, 1783, as "a cold, frosty, but bright and brilliant morning." No mention is made here of the incident of Washington's meeting the Mulligan family at table, but it is assumed, that when he reached the Battery he returned through Queen Street to the Mulligan home to fill an appointment for breakfast, accompanied probably by some member or members of his staff. The chair in which Washington sat at the Mulligan home on this occasion is still in the family, to whom it has come down from William Cooke Mulligan to his son, William, and thence to the latter's daughter, Mrs. Fanning, its present custodian. No portrait of Hercules Mulligan is known to exist. Mrs. Grace Wheeler Lawrence of New York, a descendant of Hercules through his son, John W. Mulligan, has in her possession an old blue dinner plate, and Mrs. Lawrence informs me that "this plate has come down in her family from the wife of John Mulligan, the grandson of Hercules, and that the tradition is that it was used by Washington at the Mulligan home during the Revolutionary times."

She is unable to assure me, however, that it is the identical plate which Washington used on the occasion referred to by Chief Justice Shea and John C. Hamilton. However, there can be very little doubt about it.

These mementos have been handed down in these families from generation to generation. Besides the "Washington chair," the Fanning family has also preserved many other memorials of the past which have come down from William C. Mulligan, the son of Hercules, among them an ancient bible containing entries of births, marriages and deaths, old books, portraits, letters, genealogical data, and other mementos which a proud old family usually cherishes, and it is from these interesting fragments of an intimate private family record that some of the details of this sketch have been rescued. One of the interesting items in this collection is a bound volume entirely in the handwriting of DeWitt Clinton, entitled: "Tenth Volume—Original Minutes of De Witt Clinton, [11] Mayor of the City of New York, as one of the Judges of the General Sessions of the Peace, on the trial of different indictments, from the 2nd, November 1812 to the 9th, February 1813." It bears the inscription: "Presented to John W. Mulligan by his friend, C. A. Clinton."

This in brief is the story of Hercules Mulligan. The subject is worthy of more competent treatment and I wish I could make it a more enduring memorial of the virtues and usefulness of this singular character, but it is only as good as my limited opportunities for research can make it. Why this American-Irish patriot has not been accorded a place either in the histories of the Revolution or of the City of New York I am at a loss to understand, for it is certain that less deserving historical characters of the time have been placed on a pedestal of enduring fame. It can hardly be said that the details of his career escaped the notice of the Revolutionary historians, for in gathering the materials for their work they necessarily had to consult the same sources of information that I have, and wherein, as I have shown, his name appears as an associate of some of the most eminent Americans of his time. But, despite the fact that the historians of the Revolution have ignored him, Hercules Mulligan's own countrymen are not blameless, for it is a sad but undeniable fact that the Irish in America have long neglected the memories of their unheralded heroes, while yet they have wasted their time putting the blame on the shoulders of certain historians, whose early training and environment, perhaps, may have been in an anti-Irish atmosphere.

It is indeed a standing reproach to the American-Irish that the story of such a character as Hercules Mulligan and many others of his countrymen has remained a blank for want of some suitable hand to give it currency. Such men were identified with the country's early history; they made history and they belong to history, but alas, their countrymen of the later days have not seen fit to pay them the feeblest tribute of respect or resurrect their memories from the obscurity in which they have so long been buried. If, instead of denouncing prejudiced historians, we had only gone to the original records or other sources of information, and had ourselves published our findings to the world half a century or more ago, the Irish name and race would be much more respected on this Continent than it is today.

The career of Hercules Mulligan assuredly is a lost chapter in the Revolutionary history of the City of New York; his associates were those whom the people trusted; at the dawn of the Revolution he was active, and at its close he was honored by the immortal Washington himself! Those of whom as much can be said are few indeed. But in so far as the general public is concerned, he is numbered among the unknown, "the unhonored and unsung." It is time indeed that his memory were revived and that in this City of his home some memorial should be erected to commemorate his services to the country of his adoption and his love. He is worthy of honor by all our citizens, irrespective of race or creed. He performed a most dangerous service and ran the risk of certain death if detected by the enemy, and such unselfish devotion surely merits a less obscure recognition than has been accorded him in the pages of American history. Let us hope that this son of Ireland and true American will some day receive his proper place in American history, for we have at last identified him as one of the leaders of that intrepid band of patriots who tore down and destroyed the symbol of English royalty in America, and he was but one of the thousands of his countrymen who helped to destroy and drive from these shores the last vestige of British power.

The Mulligans were fairly well represented in the American Colonies. The first known emigrant of the name recorded in this country was John Mulligan, who came to New England before 1651, in which year "John Mulligan and his wife, Elisabeth, of Scarburrugh," sold "a tract of land beginning at ye mouth of ye River called Blew Point," in what is now York County, Maine. [12] A Patrick Mulligan was listed among a large number of people who were transported from Ireland to Maryland in 1661, [13] and in the next year he was recorded as receiving four separate grants of land on the Eastern Shore of Chesapeake Bay. [14] His descendants now spell the name Mulliken and Mullican. The will of "James Mullakin or Mulligan of the Parish of Lynn Haven," dated August 22, 1668, was recorded in Lower Norfolk County, Virginia. [15] At Boston there were three distinct families, those of Hugh, John and Thomas Mulligan. Their names appear in the tax records beginning with the year 1681; the births and baptisms of their children were recorded at Boston between 1681 and 1694, [16] and in Massachusetts parish registers throughout the eighteenth century Mulligans were duly recorded. James Mulligan came from Ireland in the eighteenth century and settled at Nobleboro, Lincoln County, Maine, where he obtained a patent for a tract of land. A James Mulligan was one of several citizens of Trenton, N. J., who were adjudged "insolvent debtors" on July 5, 1765; Michael Mulligan was listed among the Chester County, Pa., "taxables" of the years 1765-1774; William Mulligan was a member of the Fifth Battalion, Chester County Militia in 1787; David Mulligan was on the tax roll of Armagh Township, Mffflin County, Pa., in 1790, [17] and among "Heads of Families" listed in the First Census (1790), we find Francis Mulligan of Charleston, Thomas and William Mulligan of Greenville County, S. C., and Alexander and Joseph Mulligan in Cheshire County, N. H.

John Mulligan, a linen merchant in Stone Street, advertised his business in the *New York Mercury* on October 26, 1767; Alexander Mulligan of New York was an importer of "Irish linens, beef, butter and other commodities" in 1768; Philip Mulligan and Jane Cammel, both of New York, were married at Trinity Church on March 12, 1776; in the baptismal registers of that church there is an entry of the baptism of "John, son of William and Ann Mulligan," on June 27, 1779, and Michael Mulligan was listed in the City Directory for 1799. John James Cluett and Sarah Mulligan were married at Trinity Church on January 20, 1780, and when their first child was baptized at that church, on St. Patrick's Day in 1782, they named her Catherine Conighane, and Francis and Margaret Conighane were the sponsors. This Francis Conighane, or Conihane as he himself spelled the name, was a lawyer and was a son of William Conihane, an Irish merchant in New York.

Apparently, none of them served in the colonial wars, and the only persons of the name listed among the soldiers and sailors of the Revolution were: Captain Francis Mulligan, commander of the privateer *Nancy* of Newport, Rhode Island; Hugh Mulligan, private in the First Regiment of the Pennsylvania Line; James Mulligan, who on April 16, 1779 , was commissioned Lieutenant of the Fourth Regiment of the Pennsylvania Line; Philip Mulligan, a private soldier in the First Regiment of the New York Line; Robert Mulligan of the Thirteenth Regiment of Albany County Militia, and John Mulligan, a soldier of the Virginia State Line. Three of them served with the Massachusetts forces, exclusive of several Mullekins and Mullicans, who I am fairly certain were descended from the Boston families before referred to. Edward Mulligan of Derry, N. H., served in Colonel John Nixon's regiment and was at the siege of Quebec on December 31, 1775, and an Edward Mulligan of Boston enlisted as a matross in Colonel Thomas Craft's Massachusetts artillery on May 21, 1776. Michael Mulligan was engaged as a seaman on the Massachusetts ship *Mars* on July 20, 1780; with others of the crew, he was sent home on a prize, but before entering Boston harbor the vessel was recaptured by the enemy; and that Michael Mulligan must have escaped or was exchanged, would appear from the fact that he was reengaged as a seaman on the Continental frigate *Deane* on December 14, 1781. Patrick Mulligan was enrolled with the Chester County, Pa., militia in 1786, and although he has been described as "a soldier of the Revolution," I am unable to find his name in the muster rolls or enlistment papers of any Revolutionary regiment.

[1] *The City of New York in the Year of Washington's Inauguration*, by Thomas E. V. Smith; New York, 1889.
[2] The original name of Cortlandt Street.
[3] *History of the Churches of New York*, by Revd. Jonathan Greenleaf; p. 333.
[4] *Annals and Occurrences of New York City and State in the Olden Times*, by John F. Watson; p. 173.
[5] Bayley, *History of the Catholic Church in New York*; p. 56.
[6] Note: At first New York Catholics worshipped in a little building at Vauxhall Gardens, near the North River between Warren and Chambers Streets, but later removed to a carpenter shop on the site of the present Saint Peter's Church in Barclay St. which was erected in 1786. For many years the officiating clergy at Saint Peter's were Irishmen. Father Whelan was succeeded by Revd. Andrew Nugent in 1786, with Revd. John Connell, an Irish Dominican, as assistant. In 1787, Revd. William O'Brien was the Pastor and Revd. Nicholas Burke from 1789 to 1793. And from the latter year down to 1806, its Pastors in succession were Revds. Matthew O'Brien, Anthony McMahon, John Byrne, Dr. Caffrey and Matthias Kelly.
[7] Some of his fellow Vestrymen in that year were Dominick Lynch, George Barnewall, Andrew Morris, John Sullivan, Charles Neylon and Patrick Farrell, and down to 1811 there are over twenty Irish names on the list of Vestrymen of Saint Peter's.
[8] This "Whalie" was Hercules Mulligan's brother-in-law, Thomas Whaly, who was a native of Donegal, Ireland. He was sexton of Trinity Church for several years.
[9] See *In Old New York*, compiled mainly from the old records of Trinity Church, by Michael J. O'Brien; New York, 1928.
[10] Vol. for 1861, p. 475.

[11] De Witt Clinton was a son of General James Clinton of the Revolution, whose father, Charles Clinton, was an immigrant from Longford, Ireland, to Orange County, New York, in the year 1731.
[12] "Book of Eastern Claims," in *Maine Historical and Genealogical Recorder;* Vol. 2.
[13] "Lists of Early Settlers"; Vol. x, at Land Commissioner's office, Annapolis, Md.
[14] Maryland Land Records; Lib. 5, fols. 56, 243-4, and 463.
[15] Probate Records; Lib. E, fol. 40.
[16] Boston Town Records.
[17] *Pennsylvania Archives.*

Chapter Thirteen

HERCULES and Elizabeth Mulligan had three sons and five daughters, all born in New York, and the following data are taken from the family papers:

Name	Date of birth	Date of death	Married
John W. Mulligan	April 13, 1774	January 17, 1862	Elizabeth Winter
Sarah Mulligan	October 12, 1775	December 8, 1810	
Elizabeth Mulligan	February 1, 1777	January 8, 1867	William Thompson
Margaret Mulligan	November 14, 1779	January 5, 1793	
William C. Mulligan	December 24, 1780	December 19, 1837	Charlotte Strong
Frances Mulligan	November 29, 1782	December 24, 1792	
Hercules Mulligan	February 8, 1785	October 1, 1785	
Mary Mulligan	May 2, 1787	December 25, 1792	

Their eldest son, John W. Mulligan, distinguished himself very early in life. In the *New York Packet* of September 28th, 1786, there was an announcement of the quarterly exercises on the next day at Columbia College Grammar School, and "all who wish to judge of the progress made there, and particularly the admirers of eloquence," were "invited to attend." The result of the oratorical contest on this occasion was thus reported in the *Packet:* "At the Quarterly examinations of Columbia College held on September 29th, the premium for eloquence was decided in favour of John W. Mulligan." The *Packet* of December 29th, 1786, also contained an account of the examinations at Columbia College for the last quarter of the year, which said that: "the premium for eloquence, *as usual,* was adjudged to Mr. John Mulligan," and another newspaper account referred to "Young Mulligan's uncommon powers of speaking, which the public have often witnessed and as often admired." When we bear in mind that John W. Mulligan was a mere boy of twelve when he won this proud distinction, we may well say that he was a phenomenal student and had before him a promising career. He graduated from Columbia in the year 1791. [1]

The *Packet* of August 15, 1788, also contained a report of "a celebration held at Flushing, Queens County, on August 8th, of the adoption of the new Constitution by a number of the inhabitants, who had collected on this occasion from different parts of the country to testify their approbation of those measures which promise happiness to us as a nation and which are so truly interesting to every one who wishes well to the rising States." The newspaper account then described the festivities, which were followed by a dinner at which "eleven toasts were drank with great enthusiasm" (eleven States having up to that time adopted the Constitution). After the toasts: "An Oration adapted to the pleasing aera was then delivered by Mr. John Mulligan, a student of Columbia College. This unexpected exhibition to the auditory, the graceful manner in which it was delivered and the truly interesting subject on which he spoke excited admiration in his hearers, and commanded loud plaudits to the youthful orator."

His career began in a public capacity. In 1793, there was much apprehension in the United States that the ill-feeling which then existed between the American and English people would lead to war. General Von Steuben was directed to make a survey of the waters surrounding the City of New York for the purpose of determining the most advantageous points on which to erect fortifications, and on March 29th, 1794, a Commission was appointed to take charge of the matter. Steuben was made President of this Commission and John W. Mulligan was chosen Secretary. Kapp, in his *Life of Baron Steuben* says: "In 1791, Steuben made the acquaintance of John W. Mulligan, a young and promising man, whose father had been an active Whig in New York City during the Revolution. Mr. Mulligan, after having finished his studies at Columbia College, became Steuben's secretary and served him with a fidelity and love which won him the friendship and confidence of his protector. Steuben concentrated all the tenderness of his heart on his friends, as he had no family relatives, and there are few examples to be found in which the feeling of kindness and good fellowship were so fully reciprocated as between Steuben and his friend." [2] In the same book, among the letters of Steuben, there is a letter from him to John W. Mulligan, dated Philadelphia, January nth, 1793, which indicates the unbroken friendship of Alexander Hamilton for this family, for the Baron began by referring to Mulligan's "Letter of the 7th, which was handed to me yesterday by Mr. Hamilton." In this letter Steuben addressed Mulligan in the most affectionate terms and consoled with him on some then recent family affliction. [3] Baron Steuben died on November 28th, 1794, and in his will [4] dated February 12, 1794, there is the following passage: "To John W. Mulligan I bequeath the whole of my library, maps and charts, and the sum of two thousand five hundred dollars to complete it."

As stated in the "Narrative of Hercules Mulligan," his son, John W., studied law in the office of Alexander Hamilton. He was admitted an attorney to the New York Bar on May 4, 1793, and opened his first office at 160 Broadway. Here, according to Barrett's *Old Merchants of New York,* [5] "he lived with his father, Hercules Mulligan, an old respected citizen during the war and many years after. He (Hercules) was one of the most fashionable merchant tailors in his day and in the war he kept at no. 23 Queen, not far from Pine. He afterwards moved to no. 3 Vesey Street. He was one of the famed Sons of Liberty. Both his sons, John W. and William C. Mulligan, were lawyers of extensive practice for many years."

In 1799 John W. Mulligan entered into partnership with Charles Brigden, with offices at number 12 Pine Street. In 1798, he married Elizabeth Winter, who is described as "a most estimable lady," and by her he had three sons, Steuben, Theodore and John W., and six daughters, Frances, Clementina, Elizabeth, Frederica, Gabriella and Mary. He became one of the leading citizens of New York in his day and was on terms of intimate friendship with Hamilton, Jay, Livingston and other distinguished men of those times. In fact, in poring over old New York records from which much of the Mulligan family data is gleaned, we are constantly in touch with the names of men who were famous in the early history of the City, merchants, professional men and politicians, whose descendants are today among the wealthiest people in Manhattan Island. During the Mayoralty of DeWitt Clinton, he was elected Assistant Alderman from the Second Ward, serving from 1806 to 1809 and during the same period, Selah Strong, whose daughter married his brother, William C. Mulligan, was the Alderman. At this period it was quite a distinction to be so honored, for only seven Aldermen constituted the entire City Council.

On October 10th, 1808, John W. Mulligan appeared before the Common Council of the City of New York, and "on application, was admitted Freeman and took the Freeman's oath." [6] On March 20th, 1810, he was elected Surrogate [7] of New York County and on March 5, 1813, he was elected County Clerk. [8] His law offices at various times were in Cedar, Liberty and Pine Streets and last at number 160 Broadway, now the home of the Lawyers' Title Insurance Company. In the published records of the Saint Nicholas' Society we find the name of John W. Mulligan on the Board of Managers from 1835 to 1840, associated with such men as Washington Irving, Peter G. Stuyvesant, Hamilton Fish, Gulian C. Verplanck, Peter Schermerhorn and other prominent citizens. In 1801, he was Master of Howard Lodge of the Royal Arch Masons, according to the City Directory of that year, and in 1803 he was a member of Erin Lodge.

In 1799 he served as Lieutenant in the 5th Regiment of New York Militia, commanded by Colonel Bernardus Swartwout, and in the next year he became its Colonel. This regiment took part in the War of 1812 as part of the 82nd Brigade of New York troops and was the last regiment employed erecting the defences of Bloomingdale Heights in 1814. Mulligan was not then in command, but that he took an active interest in military affairs during the war, is found from a reference to him in Barrett's *Old Merchants of New York,* wherein it is said that "while Mulligan was an Assistant Alderman he presented a plan for fortifying New York which Baron Steuben had drawn up, and this plan was put in force prior to the beginning of the War of 1812." [9] The number of real estate transactions in which a man figures as one of the principals usually is a safe index to his standing in the business community, and if this be accepted as a guide in the case of John W. and his brother, William C. Mulligan, we may infer that they were successful professional men. Between 1800 and 1824, John W. Mulligan appears either as grantor or grantee in eighteen title-deeds and William C. Mulligan in sixteen title-deeds, covering transfers of property in the City of New York. [10] And on the records of the Register's office there are, all told, no less than 123 legal instruments, such as conveyances, mortgages, leases, trusteeships, powers of attorney, etc., covering a period of eighty-four years after 1771, in which persons named Mulligan figured, all descendants of the Irish immigrant, Hugh Mulligan, in sixty-eight of which they are recorded as "Grantors" and in fifty-five as "Grantees."

For this period, some of these transactions were quite important from the standpoint of the extent and value of the property involved. For example, on November 4, 1800, John W. Mulligan assigned to "John Goodeve and James N. Brown, merchants of New York," for a consideration of $10,500., three bonds of $3,500, each, originally executed to John W. Mulligan by Thomas B. Brigden of New York. [11] By deed dated April 26, 1802, "Anthony Dey, Counsellor at Law of New York," conveyed to John W. Mulligan for $6,750, a house and lot on Church Street, [12] and on July 14, 1808, John W. Mulligan leased for a term of twenty-one years to Theodore F. Talbot "a parcel of land at Greenwich in the Ninth Ward of the City of New York, containing ten acres, one rood and one perch," with "the dwelling house, gardener's house, barn or stables, and the fences enclosing the said land," [13] and it was recited in the lease that this property was formerly owned by Michael Hogan, [14] who sold it to John W. Mulligan on April 1, 1807. William C. Mulligan appears in these records as the grantee in four deeds, [15] all recorded on the same day, March 26, 1811, covering the purchase by him for $6,775 of two houses and lots on Leonard, Church, Greenwich and McDougall Streets. On April 30, 1807, when only twenty-seven years of age, he was appointed to a trusteeship by Justice Daniel D. Tompkins of the Supreme Court. [16]

John W. Mulligan was associated with a number of prominent Irish citizens in the organization of the "New York Irish Emigrant Association." It was founded in 1817, with Thomas Addis Emmet as president, Daniel McCormick, vice-president, and John W. Mulligan, secretary, and in December of that year Mulligan was one of its many members who signed a "Memorial" to Congress, "to allocate lands in the Illinois Territory to be settled by Emigrants from Ireland." [17] The association still exists, as the Irish Emigrant Society and the Emigrants' Bank at 51 Chambers Street.

In politics, Mulligan was a strong Federalist. In those days the Federalists were called "Aristocrats" by their Republican opponents and the Federalists called the Republicans "Democrats," in allusion to their alleged sympathy with the Jacobins or Democrats of the French Republic. The name "Democrat" was not regularly adopted by the Party until 1829. Party politics at this period was very bitter and there were frequent personal encounters at meetings and elections. In fact, the duel between Hamilton and Burr was an outcome of these Party divisions, Hamilton having been a Federalist and Burr a Republican. John W. Mulligan was much in demand at political meetings. He was a man of vigorous and cultivated intellect, with a great flow of language and impassioned oratory, and, as we are informed, "he was for many years one of the most popular men in the City" and "no man took a more active part in public affairs than Mr. Mulligan." [18]

Several references to John W. Mulligan may be found in historical works relating to the City of New York during the early years of the last century. One of the most entertaining stories dealing with this period is that told by Dr. John W. Francis of the New York Historical Society, in a paper read before that body in the year 1838 and which was published in 1866 under the title of "Old New York, or Reminiscences of the Past Sixty Years." Dr. Francis was a leading New York physician and the holder of important offices in connection with public charities and literary and scientific societies, and his "Reminiscences" are remarkable for the amount of information they contain relative to old New York. He relates that for several years after the Revolution "the City still retained a vast number of the Tory party, who, while they were ready to be the participators of the benefits of that freedom which sprung out of the Revolution, were known to be dissatisfied by the mortifications of defeat under which they still writhed"; that "the true Whigs, the rebel phalanx so to speak, were often circumscribed in thought and in utterance by the actions of the tory element." Even as late as 1804, such bad feeling existed between the tories and the patriots, that the former on several occasions tried to prevent the holding of public meetings at which the Declaration of Independence was read and where the wrongs endured by the patriots under the colonial government were recounted. Dr. Francis, in referring to one of those meetings, held in New York on the 4th of July, 1804, says: "I witnessed a turmoil which arose upon the occasion of the expressed sentiments of the orator of the day, John W. Mulligan, Esq., now, I believe, the oldest living graduate of Columbia College." The fact that John W. Mulligan was selected as "the orator of the day" on this occasion in itself indicates the important place occupied by him among the citizens of New York, at a time when many of the leading patriots of the Revolution were still active in business and in the politics of the State and Nation.

According to the *Commercial Advertiser* of July 5, 1804, Mulligan's oration was delivered at the Brick Presbyterian Church. With regard to the "turmoil" referred to by Dr. Francis, it appears that Mulligan in his remarks offended some of the Democrats who were present, and the *Commercial Advertiser* in commenting on the speech, said: "The displeasure of the Democrats with Mr. Mulligan for his oration delivered before them on the late anniversary of Independence, is unaccountable by all not acquainted with the principles which actuated them. The prominent feature of the oration was an encomium on the administration of President Washington. Why should this offend them? To pass by the masterly performance, without a tributary remark on the style and manner in which it was written and delivered, would be doing injustice to the orator and to our feelings. The sentiments were those of

1776, couched in the glowing language of a patriot and American...the ebullitions of a sound heart and correct judgment and dictated solely by a pure and ardent love of country."

[1] *Catalogue of the Officers and Graduates of Columbia University,* published by the University, 1906.
[2] *Life of Frederick William von Steuben, Major-General of the Revolutionary Army,* by Frederick Kapp, with an introduction by Bancroft; New York, 1859.
[3] Probably the death of his sister Margaret, who died only two days before his letter to Steuben.
[4] Will on file and recorded in the Office of the Court of Appeals and of the Secretary of State at Albany, Recorded *ut supra,* p. 460.
[5] Vol, 1, p. 365.
[6] *Collections,* New York Historical Society; Vol. for 1885, p. 366.
[7] In the Surrogate's records there are entries of several decrees admitting wills to probate, signed by "John W. Mulligan, Surrogate." The earliest is dated April 6, 1810, in connection with the will of Anne Elder of New York (Lib. 48, p. 419).
[8] *Civil List and Constitutional History of the Colony and State of New York;* by Stephen C. Hutchins, p. 397; Albany, 1883.
[9] *Old Merchants of New York;* Vol. 1, p. 411.
[10] Records of Conveyances at the Register's office of the City and County of New York.
[11] *Ibid.,* Lib. 59, p. 276.
[12] *Ibid.,* Lib. 196, p. 91.
[13] *Ibid.,* Lib. 80, p. 474.
[14] Michael Hogan was a New York merchant and at one time was United States Consul at Havana, Cuba. He was a native of County Clare, Ireland. He was the owner of a large tract of land on the northern end of Manhattan Island, and it was he who named Claremont on Riverside Drive, now one of the finest residential sections of the City of New York, after his native County in Ireland. Between 1800 and 1812, Michael Hogan appears in the records of the Register's Office of New York City and County as the grantor in twelve legal instruments. A tablet to his memory may be seen at Grace Church, Broadway and Tenth Street.
[15] Lib. 91, pp. 319, 322 and 325.
[16] Two other Trustees were Owen Flanagan and John W. Van Orden.
[17] *New York's First Emigrant Society,* by Thomas F. Meehan; in United States Catholic Historical Society; Vol. 6, part 2, pp. 202-211.
[18] Barrett's *Old Merchants of New York;* Vol. 1.

Chapter Fourteen

JOHN W. MULLIGAN'S daughter, Frances, married a Revd. Mr. Hill about 1831, and "she and her sister, Frederica, accompanied Mr. Hill to Athens, where the great American Mission School under their charge became so celebrated." [1] As a matter of fact, according to the family records, the Mulligan girls themselves were the founders of this school. After the death of his wife. Mulligan also went to Greece and was United States Consul at Athens for several years. He died at New York on January 17th, 1862, and the *New York Commercial,* in closing its obituary of him, paid him this excessive, but probably well-meant, tribute: "We shall never see his like again!" A full copy of the notice here follows:

"Died; On Friday, January 17th., John W. Mulligan, Esq., in the 88 th. year of his age. The relatives and friends are invited to attend the funeral from the Church of the Incarnation, corner of Madison Avenue and 28 th. Street, without further invitation this afternoon at three o'clock.

"The subject of the above notice was born in New York while New York was under British rule, but he well remembered and often related how he stood as a little boy on a hill where Grand Street now crosses Broadway and saw the last British sentinel file off on the memorable 25th of November. He graduated from Columbia College and afterwards practiced law. Governor King was a student in his office. At one time he was a member of Baron Steuben's family and assisted at his interment. He was acquainted with Jay and Hamilton, as well as with other distinguished men of those times, and partook of their strong Federalist views. In religion, he was an Episcopalian—a Churchman. Some years ago, he had the pleasure of visiting Athens, and seeing the fruits of his labors for the cause of Christ in the school founded by his daughters, Mrs Hill and Frederica Mulligan. His manners were urbane, in his conversation remarkably interesting, his memory being good to the last. We shall never see his like again."

His sons, Steuben and Theodore, died at sea and the family are unable to furnish any information concerning them. John W. Mulligan, Junior, was born on January 4, 1812, and died on August 13, 1853. His name appears in the New York City Directories between 1835 and 1850 as a commission and dry goods merchant at various times in Nassau, Gold, Pearl and Liberty Streets. He married Susan Halleck, of the same family as FitzGreene Halleck, the American poet. They had two sons, John and William, and a daughter, Annie, who married Andrew C. Wheeler, the famous humorist, best known to the public as "Nym Crinkle," and who was, perhaps the greatest American dramatic critic of his time. Mrs. Grace Wheeler Lawrence, who prizes the possession of the "Washington Plate," is a daughter of "Nym Crinkle." She is very proud of her Irish lineage and especially of her descent from the Revolutionary patriot, and she recalls her mother often relating a story, "how people were fascinated by the handsome young Irishman in knee breeches, with silver buckles on his shoes." The subject of this little story was Hercules Mulligan, and although only eleven years old at the time of his death, Mrs. Wheeler distinctly remembered the appearance of the aged man and of the stories handed down in the family of his friendship with Alexander Hamilton and his activities as one of the "Liberty Boys."

William C. Mulligan, the second son of Hercules, was born on December 4, 1780. On April 13, 1813, he married a beautiful woman, Charlotte Strong, daughter of a New York merchant named Selah Strong, who, in 1802 was Comptroller of the City. Six sons were born to this union, Henry Strong, William, Edward, Alfred, Eugene and Romeyn Mulligan. Like his brother, he was a successful lawyer and was in business in Cedar, Pine and William Streets at various times. He was a member of the old Presbyterian Church in Cedar Street between Nassau and William, founded in 1807 by Selah Strong and others, and of which Dr. John B. Romeyn was the first pastor. This was the beginning of the present Fifth Avenue Presbyterian Church, and in the published histories of that Church there are on its lists of members a number of people named Mulligan, who, doubtless, were descendants of the Revolutionary patriot. William C. Mulligan was also a charter member of the American Bible Society on its organization in 1816. [2] He died on November 19th, 1837, and his will, recorded at the office of the Surrogate for New York County, [3] indicates him to have been a man of considerable wealth. He was buried in the vault of the Strong family in Saint Mark's churchyard, where also were buried his sons, Edward and Eugene.

The descendants of William C. Mulligan were very refined people. His eldest son, Henry Strong Mulligan, born March 5, 1815, is said to have been "an exceedingly handsome, finely set-up man," who travelled a great deal in Europe. He was a well known art connoisseur and collector of curios and filled his home with such objects. On September 5, 1839, he married Sally Chapin Howell of Canandaigua, N. Y., daughter of Nathaniel W. Howell, who was the first Judge of Ontario County. They had six children. He appears in the City Directory for several years as a merchant in Pearl Street, and in 1847, in which year his name appears for the last time, he was at 166 Front Street and resided at Astoria, Long Island. He was an Elder of the Presbyterian Church, formerly at Duane and Church Streets, of which Revd. George Potts was Pastor, and his name is recorded as one of twenty subscribers, who in 1844 agreed "to purchase the ground at the corner of Wooster and Fourth Streets, and build a church to be placed under the care of Mr. Potts." This agreement resulted in the erection in 1845 of the present edifice of the University Place Presbyterian Congregation, and among its subscribers may be found the names of some of the leading New York families of the time.

Henry Strong Mulligan's eldest son, James Strong Mulligan, was a Lieutenant in the United States Army and died at Buffalo, N. Y., on June 9th, 1863, of wounds received at the battle of Bull Run. In the genealogy of the Strong family he is thus referred to:

"James Strong Mulligan, born July 6th, 1840; Lieutenant, 21st Regiment, New York State Militia; entered United States Army volunteers as a private in Company B, 21st Regiment, at the beginning of the war and became in the end First Lieutenant of Company I; engaged in many skirmishes in Northern Virginia. At the second battle of Bull Run, the command of his company early devolved upon him and while in a terrible cross-fire he was struck by a bullet, which at the time he supposed had only gone through his arm, and he continued on in the fight until the enemy was driven back, and his company recalled, when he fell from loss of blood and it was found that the ball had passed through his left lung out under the shoulder. He was made prisoner by the enemy, stripped and left on the field for several days, attended only by a faithful soldier of his company who would not desert him. On being recovered at last by his friends he was removed to Washington and in November to his home in Buffalo, and tenderly cared for, but unavailingly, and died June 9th, 1863, a brave Christian soldier. His regiment returned to Buffalo in the Spring of 1863 and marched by his mother's house in order to show their respect for their old wounded and dying officer, and as he was brought out on the balcony to see them for the last time, greeted him with cheers and uplifted hats." [4]

Henry Strong Mulligan's second son, Greig Howell Mulligan, was also an officer in the United States Army during the Civil War. He first joined the 21st Regiment with his brother, James, but in 1861 was made Lieutenant of Company A, 90th Regiment of New York Volunteers, and died at Key West, Fla., on August 22, 1862. He is described as "the most thorough officer in the regiment, very able and brilliant and a warm-hearted, generous friend." [5] The third child of Henry Strong Mulligan was Charlotte, who was born in New York on September 25, 1844, and who died at Buffalo on June 20th, 1900, lamented by a large circle of friends and admirers. The fourth was Morris Howell, who died in infancy; the fifth was Henry Strong Mulligan, Junior, who married Elizabeth Haddock at Buffalo in 1877, and the last was Edward Howell Mulligan, born at Buffalo on November 12, 1852, whose home was at Pasadena, California. Some years ago Mr. Edward H. Mulligan went to Ireland, for the purpose of tracing the ancestry of his great-grandfather, but without success, and he was there informed that all the old records of the family probably were destroyed.

William, second son of William C. Mulligan, born July 4, 1817, married Ellen Wikoff of Philadelphia. He was a New York merchant and became president in 1862 of the Humboldt Fire Insurance Company. Their children were: Julia Strong, Caroline Park, Charlotte Wikoff, Annie Tharp and Ellen Wikoff Mulligan. The first three died unmarried. Annie Tharp Mulligan married Dr. Samuel B. Smallwood of Newbern, N. C., and they resided at Huntington, Long Island, where two children were born to them, Annie and William Mulligan Smallwood. Ellen Wikoff Mulligan married Robert Fanning, son of Patrick Fanning of Norwich, Conn. They lived at Astoria and Flushing, Long Island, and she died at the latter place in 1934 at the age of eighty-five. Her daughters still reside in Flushing.

Edward, third son of William C. Mulligan, born March 31, 1819, died at the age of fourteen. Alfred, the fourth son, born February 21, 1821, married Julia Grant Prince and resided at Huntington, Long Island. Their children were: Mary Prince, Virginia, Frederick, William, Eugene Livingston and Francis Mulligan, some of whose descendants still reside on Long Island.

Eugene, fifth son of William C. Mulligan, married (1) Harriet Rich of Buffalo and (2) Sophia McCay of Bath, New York, and he was the father of Mary Evelyn, Florence and Jeannie McCay Mulligan. Mary Evelyn married Charles Townsend of New York, and their daughter, Mrs. Louise Townsend Lord, resides at Morristown, New Jersey. Romeyn, youngest son of William C. Mulligan, born January 31, 1828, married Maria Louisa Holden of Batavia, New York, and they were the parents of Delia and Romeyn Mulligan.

Charlotte, daughter of Henry Strong Mulligan and great-granddaughter of Hercules Mulligan, was a remarkable woman. In her youth she removed with her parents to Buffalo, and from a published account of her activities in that City in later years we obtain some interesting data. The death of her brother, James, after his return from the Civil War badly wounded, had a great effect on the young girl, and, as she stated to one of her earliest friends, "I decided then that I would devote my life to doing something for men." She faithfully kept her word. She was the founder of an organization in Buffalo, known as "The Guard of Honor," an institution which for more than half a century did splendid work in the care and education of boys and the securing of employment for unfortunate men. As an evidence of her characteristic modesty and self-effacement, the *Century Magazine* for May, 1880, contains an article on "The Guard of Honor," contributed by her at the request of the editor, Richard Watson Gilder, in which she entirely refrained from saying that she had any connection with the institution and took none of the credit of its great work on herself!

Miss Elizabeth M. Howe, who knew her intimately, writes of her: "As we study Miss Mulligan's activities, we see that two main ideas controlled her gift of leadership. The first was exemplified in the Guard of Honor, 'er firstling,' her life-inspiration to which all things were subsidiary and for which she worked and sacrificed with unfaltering constancy. This work called into play the instinct for helpfulness which was one of her deepest qualities. Its expression was almost universal; the searching glance of her fine eyes, the warmth of her hand-clasp, her cordial voice, all proclaimed it. She had great understanding of human nature, she was buttressed by common sense and deeply motived by religion. From these qualities sprang her great power over the individual, which found its fullest expression in her dealings with the men of the Guard of Honor. They still hold an annual meeting in memory of her!"

Charlotte Mulligan has been described as "the pioneer woman philanthropist of Western New York" and many charitable institutions adopted her methods for their model, and it is said that Edward Everett Hale's story, *Mrs. Merriam's Scholars,* was founded on her work. To the poor and the needy, regardless of religious affiliations, she gave freely of her means; she was ever devoted to the common good and in the language of one of her friends, "thousands of other lives drew strength and guidance from her heroic example!" It is interesting to find that in many of the American descendants of the Irish Bardic family of O'Mulligan a love for music and literature has been one of their prominent characteristics, especially in the Mulligan girls, and Charlotte Mulligan strongly exhibited this trait in her early youth. For several years she was the soprano in the First Church and at Calvary Church in Buffalo, and after a year's study in Philadelphia she went to Europe and studied singing under the famous Madame Marchesi. While in Paris an incident occurred that showed her quick decision and power to do the right thing at the right moment. "She was sitting in a church listening to a difficult and beautiful aria by the soprano, when the singer was seen to turn ghastly pale and tottered a little. In an incredibly short time Miss Mulligan had found her way into the choir, had taken the girl's place, taken up the note as she left it, and went on and finished this beautiful thing in her rich, wonderful voice!"

On her return to Buffalo, she established a musical school. At her attractive home in Johnson Park, which was for years the Mecca of the best people of the City, she gave musicales and social entertainments, as well as free lessons in vocal and instrumental music to those unable to meet the expense of such training. She is said to have been "one of the first women in Buffalo to take up newspaper work." In the early seventies she joined the staff of the Buffalo *Courier* as musical critic, holding that position until within a year or two of her death in 1900. "During this time," writes one of her friends, "she became interested in all other women who wrote either for the press or periodicals and in 1893 she established the club known as 'The Scribblers,' which has remained until the present time a prosperous organization." In 1894, she founded the famous woman's organization of Buffalo known as "The Twentieth Century Club," which she dedicated "to education, literature and art." This remarkable woman died at her summer home at Cloverbank, on the shore of Lake Erie, on June 20th, 1900, and at her funeral, we are told, "all Buffalo turned out to do her honor." In testimony of the affectionate regard in which the citizens of Buffalo cherished her memory, the Twentieth Century Club, fourteen years after her death, held a memorial meeting in her honor, and it is from the published report of this meeting and of the beautiful tributes paid to her memory by the women of Buffalo on that occasion that the foregoing details concerning Charlotte Mulligan are obtained.

[1] Barrett's *Old Merchants of New York.*
[2] *History of the Fifth Avenue Presbyterian Church,* by W. Jessup; New York; 1909.
[3] Liber 78, p. 62.
[4] *The History of the Descendants of John Strong of Northampton, Mass.,* by Benjamin W. Dwight; Vol. i, p. 713; Albany, 1871.
[5] Strong Genealogy.

Appendices

Appendix One - To Charlotte Mulligan
[A]
(Great-granddaughter of Hercules Mulligan, born in New York, September 25th, 1844. Died at Buffalo, N. Y., June 20, 1900.)

HER heart was great with goodness, she foresaw
The world as God's world, rich in hidden power;
All her brave days, aye, each full-freighted hour
Proved her wide vision, learned of Love's deep law;
From fathomless wells of faith her soul did draw
Those healing draughts she made her brother's dower.
And dauntless, dared, and never did she cower
To do, not dream high deeds without a flaw.

O, Master-Woman, thy dynamic mind
Was crystal clear, yet warm with tenderness;
What voice may chant, what fervent pen express
Thy lofty soul, thy service, nobly kind?
Lo, gleaming in these countless hearts we find
Thy fadeless coronal, great Prophetess!

[A] Composed by Mrs. Alfred G. Hauenstein, and read at the Memorial Meeting of the Twentieth Century Club at Buffalo, N. Y., November 9th, 1914.

Appendix Two - Breakfast with Hercules Mulligan

By Shaemas O'Sheel.
[B]

THE last red file of grenadiers halts at the grey sea-wall,
They have crowded into the last long boat that scarcely holds them all,
And the sullen oarsmen pull for the ships that shall sail and never return,
And the Union Jack of Britain droops, dejected, at the stern.
And now as the night's grey fleece is shorn by the golden shears of the sun,
Slowly, astride his dappled grey,
Down to the Battery, down to the Bay,
Riding, comes Washington.

His aides-de-camp
Hold back the throng
As he reins his dappled grey,
And notes how the white sails take the breeze
And the black ships slink from the Bay.
Now sped by the sun's bright arrows
They have vanished beyond the Narrows,
And they'll come not back through the Narrows
This side of Judgment Day.

And the people's shout is mighty,
And all eyes turn as one
To the dappled grey and its rider,
The silent Washington.
But 'Washington broods apart;
His thoughts go back through the years
That heard no clamorous cheers
To ease disaster's smart.
The pageant unrolls before him
Of the days that tried and tore him,
When only faith upbore him.
And only the valiant heart.
What wonder that he can scarcely see
The radiant face of victory
As the last ship slinks away to the sea
And the last link falls
Of the chain that galls
The newborn daughter of Liberty?

The last tall mast has faded away;
Washington turns on the dappled grey.
And bows to a silent rider near him,
Speaking loudly that all may hear him,
"Hercules Mulligan, if I may,
I will break my fast with you this day!"

Over the Bowling Green they ride,
Washington, Mulligan, side by side;
Thus the Chieftain, in all men's view
Proves Hercules Mulligan staunch and true.

For Washington knows the Irish breed;
They sprung to arms in the hour of need,
Sullivan, first to strike on land,
O'Brien, first to strike at sea,
Knox and Moylan and Wayne and Hand,
Barry, Magaw and Shee.
They proved their mettle on many a field.
First to charge and last to yield,
In the cause of Liberty.

Washington smiles and bows to his host;
"Hercules Mulligan, here's a toast:
If the land we have seen this day set free
Ever shall be in danger From foe within or stranger.
May Heaven grant, to save us then,
The hearts and the hands of Irishmen."
And the shout rings 'round the board, "Amen"!

[B] Read by the author at a memorial meeting in honor of Hercules Mulligan, at Fraunces' Tavern, New York, on December 3, 1932.

Appendix Three - Narrative of Hercules Mulligan

(Document number 13,695 in the "Papers of Major-General Alexander Hamilton," in the Department of Manuscripts, Library of Congress)

Photostat of Original

to his entire satisfaction. Mr Hamilton then stated that he wished to enter either of the classes to which his attainments would entitle him but with the understanding that he should be permitted to advance from Class to Class with as much rapidity as by his own exertion he would be enable him to do Dr Witherspoon listened with great attention to so unusual a proposition from so young a person and replied that he had not the power to determine but that he would submit the request to the trustees who would decide which was done and in about a fortnight after a letter was received from the President stating that the request could not be complied with because it was contrary to the usage of the Colledge and in: fusing his regret because he was assured that the young gentleman would do him to any sem: inary at which he should be educated

That he then entered Kings (now Columbia) Colledge on the same plan & $ on the diploma plan he had proposed at Princeton and boarded with my family &

While in Colledge He formed a voluntier company which was commanded by Capt Fleming It having been determin: ed by the Committee of Safety that the Cannon which were in the Battery should be removed to a place of greater safety This Cur hears with others was engaged in making the removal when (28 augt 75.) The Asia fired upon the City and I recollect well that Mr Hamilton was there for I was engaged in hawling off one

89

of the Cannon when Mr. H came up and gave me his musket to hold & he took hold of the rope The front of the Asia that had before approached near the Battery and was sent who and a man was killed He returned to the Park and — It. Son was there opened who as Hamilton was at that time away with the Cannon I fired a shell from his musket a returned to him as he was returning I met him and he asked when his piece was I told him where I had left it and he went for it not withstanding the firing continued with as much unconcern as if the Vessel had not been there About the 10 or 12 July 1776 Mr. Hamilton being desirous to enter the Army & a Commission as a Capt. of Artillery was promised to him on the Condition that he should raise thirty men himself with his that very afternoon I came and we engaged 25 men the next day a return was made to the Convention & recommendation was unanimously prepared and the Commission in due form Hamilton mounted his men and with his own funds equipped the the attended to their drill and his other duties with a degree of zeal and diligence which soon made his Company conspicuous for their attendance and the regularity of their movements

I KNEW Alexander Hamilton shortly after his arrival in the City of New York from the West Indies whence he sailed to Boston and thence came here in the month of October 1773. He brought letters from the Revd. Mr. Knox of St. Croix to Guverner Livingston, Mr. Boudinot, Dr. Rogers and others and one to the House of Kortright and Co. Merchants of the City of New York (my brother was the Company) to whom was also assigned from time to time the first shortly after his arrival West India Produce to be sold and the proceeds to be applied to his use.

I understood from him that he wrote two or three political pieces -while he was at Boston which were published in a newspaper there. He first went to a grammar school at Elizabeth town kept by a Mr. Barber before he had been there one year he told me and I was also informed of the same by a letter from the teacher that he was prepared to enter Colledge. He came to N.Y., and told me he preferred Princeton to Kings Colledge because it was more republican. I went with him to Princeton to the House of Dr. Witherspoon the then president of the Colledge with whom I was well acquainted and I introduced Mr. Hamilton to him and proposed to him to examine the young gentleman which the Doctor did to his entire satisfaction. Mr. Hamilton then stated that he wished to enter either of the classes to which his attainments would entitle him but with the understanding that he should be permitted to advance from Class to Class with as much rapidity as his exertions would enable him to do. Dr. Witherspoon listened with great attention to so unusual a proposition from so young a person and replied that he had not Jie power to determine but that he would submit the request to the trustees who would decide which was done and in about a fortnight after a letter was received from the President stating that the request could not be complied with because it was contrary to the usage of the Colledge and expressing his regret because he was convinced that the young gentleman would do honor to any seminary at which he should be educated.

He then entered Kings (now Columbia Colledge) in the Spring of *7 5 in the Sophomore Class and at the terms he had proposed at Princeton and boarded with my family.

While in Colledge he joined a volunteer uniform company which was commanded by Capt. Fleming. It having been determined by the Committee of Safety that the Cannon which were on the Battery should be removed to a place of greater safety this Company with others were engaged in making the removal when (28 Augt 75) The Asia fired upon the City and I recollect well that Mr. Hamilton was there for I was engaged in hauling off one of the Cannon when Mr. H. came up and gave me his musket to hold and he took hold of the rope. The Boat of the Asia had before approached the Battery and was fired upon and a man was killed. She returned to the ship and the fire was then opened upon us. Hamilton at the first firing was away with the Cannon I left his musket in the battery and retreated as he was returning I met him and he asked for his piece I told him where I had left it and he went for it notwithstanding the firing continued with as much unconcern as if the Vessel had not been there.

About the 10 or 12 July 1776 Mr. Hamilton being desirous to enter the Army a Commission as a Capt. of Artillery was promised to him on the Condition that he should raise thirty men I went with him that very afternoon and we engaged 25 men, the next day a report was made to the Committee and a recommendation was unanimously passed and the Commission was obtained. Hamilton recruited his men and with his own funds equiped them.

He attended to their drill and his other duties with a degree of zeal and diligence which soon made his Company conspicuous for their appearance and the regularity of their movements. About this time the first division of the British Army arrived at Sandy Hook Capt. Hamilton went on the Battery with his Company and his piece of artillery and commenced a Brisk fire upon the Phoenix and Rose then sailing up the river when his cannon burst and killed two of his men who I distinctly recollect were buried in the Boling Green.

Previously to the Skirmish on Long Island Mr. H. The Revd John Mason father of the present Dr. Mason were at Dinner at my House and after others (perhaps Mr Rhinelander & Col Lamb) had retired from the table they were lamenting the situation of the army on Long Island and suggesting the best plans for its removal when Mr. Mason and Mr. Hamilton determined to write an anonymous letter to Genl Washington pointing out their ideas of the best means to draw off the Army I saw Mr. H writing the letter & heard it read after it was finished It was delivered to me to be handed to one of the family of the General and I gave it to Col Webb then an aid De Champ and I have no doubt he delivered it because my impression at that time was that the mode of Drawing off the army which was adopted was nearly the same as that pointed out in the letter.

When, the enemy came in the City on Sunday at 8 O'clock Capt. H commanded a post on Bunker Hill near New York and fought with the rear of our army and in returning he lost as he afterwards told Me his baggage and one of his Cannon which broke down.

After the British crossed the Hudson at Fort Lee I went to see my young friend and found him encamped near Genl. Washington having the command of his Company. I afterwards saw him when he came to New York with a flag to see Sir Guy Carlton. He evinced his gratitude for the attentions of my brother & myself by his attentions to us through life & by taking one of my sons to study Law without charging the least compensation.

While Mr. Hamilton was at Colledge he wrote several Political essays and in 1776 he wrote the Westchester Farmer Refuted in my house and a part in my presence and read some of the pages to me as he wrote then. At the time this publication was attributed to Gouvnr Livingston...Mr H used in the evenings to sit with my family and my brother's family and write dogerel rhymes for their amusement he was all ways amiable and Cheerful and extremely attentive to his books.

When Rivington's Press was attacked by a Company from the Eastward Mr. H indignant that our neighbours should intrude upon our rights (although the press was considered a tory one) he went to the place addressed the people present and offered if any others would join him to prevent these intruders from taking the types away.

Dr. Cooper President of Kings Colledge was a tory and an obnoxious man and the mob went to the Colledge with the intention of tarring and feathering him or riding him upon a rail Mr. H got on the stoop of the President's house and harangued them in order to give him time to escape out of the back of the House which he did & went on Board a Frigate Lying in the North river.

Endorsed: "Hercules Mulligan's narrative respecting the early life of A. H.

---

about the time the first division of the British army arrived at Sandy Hook Capt Hamilton went on the Battery with his Company and his piece of artillery and commenced a Brisk fire upon the Phoenix and Rose then passing up the river when his Cannon burst and killed two of his men who I distinctly recollect were buried in the Bowling Green

Previously to the Phoenix & Rose Long Island Mr H. & the Revd John Mason father of the present Dr Mason were at dinner at my House and after others (perhaps Mr Rhinelander & Col Trunk) had retired from the table they were lamenting the situation of the army on Long Island and suggesting the best plans for its removal when Mr Mason and Mr Hamilton determined to write an anonymous letter to Genl Washington pointing out their ideas of the best means to draw off the army. I saw Mr H. writing the letter & heard it read after it was finished It was delivered to me to be handed to some one of the family of the General and I gave it to Col Webb. He received it & Channed and I have no doubt he delivered it because my impression at that time was that the mode of drawing off the army which was adopted was nearly the same as that pointed out in the letter

When the enemy came in the City on sunday at 8 Oclock Capt H. commanded a fort on

Bunker Hill near New York and brought off with the rear of our army and in returning he lost as he afterwards told me his baggage — and one of his Cannon which broke down

After the British crossed the Hudson at Fort Lee I went to see my young friend and found him encamped near Gen'l Washington having the Command of his Company — I afterwards saw him when he came to New York with a flag to see Sir Guy Carlton he evinced his gratitude for the attentions of my brother & myself, by his attentions to us through life by taking one of my sons to study law without charging the least compensation

While Mr Hamilton was at Colledge he wrote several Political essays and in 1776 he wrote the Westchester Farmer refuted in my house and a part in my presence and read some of the pages to me as he wrote them. at the time this publication was attributed to Gov'r Livingston ——— Mr H. used in the evening, to sit with my family and my brother family and write doggerel rhymes for their amusement he was always amiable and Cheerful and extremely attentive to his book.

When Rivington's Press was attacked by a Company from the Eastward Mr H indignant that an enough tories should intrude upon our rights (although the press was considered a tory one) he went to the place addressed the people present and offered if any other would join him to prevent them intruders from taking the types away

Dr Cooper President of the Kings Colledge

was a tory and an obnoxious man and the mob went to the College with the intention of tarring & feathering him a riding him upon a rail. Mr H got a [?] of [?] the Presidents house and harangued them in order to give him time to escape out of the back of the house which he did & went on board a Frigate lying in the North river

Hercules Mulligan
narrative respecting the
early life of A H

CPSIA information can be obtained
at www.ICGtesting.com
Printed in the USA
BVHW081433030522
635996BV00031B/2150